to work

This series is commissioned by the Institute of Management Foundation.

Putting Assertiveness to Work

A programme for management excellence

■ ■ ■

GRAHAM WILLCOCKS &
STEVE MORRIS

the Institute of Management
FOUNDATION
PITMAN PUBLISHING

London · Hong Kong · Johannesburg
Melbourne · Singapore · Washington DC

PITMAN PUBLISHING
128 Long Acre, London WC2E 9AN
Tel: +44 (0)171 447 2000
Fax: +44 (0)171 240 5771

A Division of Pearson Professional Limited

First published in Great Britain 1996

British Library Cataloguing in Publication Data
A CIP catalogue record for this book can be obtained from the British Library.

ISBN 0 273 62331 1

10 9 8 7 6 5 4 3 2 1

Typeset by Pantek Arts, Maidstone, Kent
Printed and bound in Great Britain by Bell and Bain Ltd, Glasgow

The Publishers' policy is to use paper manufactured from sustainable forests.

About the Authors

Graham Willcocks is director of Wesley House Consultancy. He is a writer, trainer and process consultant. He has had wide management experience in both the private and public sectors, developing programmes on leadership, teams, change, customer care and strategic marketing within a wide range of organisations.

Steve Morris, director of The Burton Morris Consultancy, is an experienced writer of books, articles and action guides on management. He works with a range of organisations such as The National Consumer Council, Ind Coope, Forte Posthouse and TSB. He is learning consultant for the Institute of Personnel and Development, the University of London and the University of the West Indies.

Contents

Acknowledgements x

Introduction xi

1 The background to assertiveness 1

High-tech world: low-tech problems 1
What assertiveness is and how it helps 2
The acid test 4
Working in the hot-house 4
The organisation and you 6
Personal development 6
The manager's day at Hades Incorporated 8
Life at Nirvana Corporation 9
Moving on ... 13
Working in the real world 14
Saying 'No' 18
The obvious places where conflict occurs 20
The less obvious places 21
Taking flight 24
Fight 25
The makings of a better manager 29

2 I'm really sorry, but I hate you 31

Assertiveness matters 31
What assertiveness means to you 32
Assertiveness is not a quick fix 35
Understanding your personal style 36
Who am I? 37
Passive or submissive? 40
And you? 42
The effects of passive behaviour on individuals 43
The effects of passive behaviour on the organisation 43
Possum's law 44
Aggressive behaviour 47
The effects of aggressive behaviour on individuals 48

The effects of aggressive behaviour on the organisation 49
Manipulative behaviour 53
Aiming for win–win using assertive behaviour 55
Winning through assertiveness 57
Some heretical thoughts 60
And finally ... handling the aftermath of conflict 61

3 Where are you now? 65

Doing the diagnostic 65
You and your manager 66
Saying 'No' (or 'Yes' when you want to) 68
Conquering the fear of being disliked 72
Stating your point of view 78
Handling unexpected conflict 84
Preparing to handle a difficult situation 86
Where to now? 87

4 Assertiveness – taking those first steps 91

Getting started 91
Understanding rights and responsibilities 92
The right to be wrong 95
Where to now? 96
The assertiveness ABC 97
Putting the ABC into action 110
Dealing with colleagues 115
Getting started 118
Saying 'No' 119
Offering solutions to difficult situations 120
Giving praise 121
Accepting praise 122
Listen first; react after 122

5 Negotiating – a skill for all seasons 125

What is negotiation? 127
Mutual interests and trade-offs 128
The outcomes of negotiation 132
The process of negotiation 135
Five steps in negotiation 136
Preparation 137
Invitation 140
Presentation 142

Give and take 143
Closing the deal 150
Will principled negotiation always work? 151
Resolving conflict using negotiation 151

6 Staying in control 155

Controlling the process 156
Clouding the issue 161
Where are we now? 165
Giving feedback assertively 166

7 Moving ahead 175

Some further techniques 175
Assertive thinking 176
Stating feelings 178
What matters most 181
Trying techniques out in safety 187
Reviewing how you got on 194
Planning for the future 197
Personal review and action plan 198

A final thought 201

Index 205

Acknowledgements

The authors would like to thank Sue McKoen for drafting parts of this book.

Introduction

When we first encountered assertiveness as a management topic we were sceptical. Our initial thoughts were that it was something for special-interest groups, because at the time assertiveness was something of a new fashion. It had the feel of something a bit soft and, frankly, a touch 'hippy'. Surely this wasn't a serious management issue?

How wrong can one be!

Not unnaturally, given our initial feelings about it, we took some convincing. So we studied the subject, related the theory to our real lives, and we tried it out for ourselves. The first step was the hardest – accepting that assertiveness is more than a few tricks and techniques. But then it dawned that any improvement in personal or management behaviour is primarily based on attitude, beliefs and values. Whether it's total quality management, business process re-engineering or customer care, nothing sticks unless it comes from a belief within. Applying sticking plasters and going for quick fixes never made it better for long.

So we discussed it and came to the view that ... yes, we did feel we had the right to express our real feelings and have them listened to, and ... yes, we also had the responsibility of listening to others. One key problem in the past had been that we often felt a bit passive, inhibited from telling other people unwelcome truths, even though putting a good gloss on things changed absolutely nothing. If there wasn't time to do a job, saying that we'd do our best still didn't change the facts of the situation. All it did was lead to disappointment, overwork, a sense of failure and potential lost business in future. We wanted to change that.

We also wanted to avoid the possibility of coming across as aggressive, of putting other people in the position where *they* felt inhibited about speaking out and telling us what we needed to know – the truth about situations. If we were guilty of that, then we lost out as much as they did from being passive, as our approach meant others were agreeing to unrealistic or irrelevant targets.

Having accepted that assertiveness is a philosophy that says we have these two-way rights and responsibilities, we then looked at the techniques and started to try them out. The impact was quite amazing. We had to admit within a few days that we were total converts. The secret of our conversion was that this is a topic that is simply about staying in control of what you say and how you say it; there's no magic formula, but equally, there's no need to undergo a personality change.

Our experience showed us that we got better results from transactions with suppliers, clients, colleagues and each other. Our stress levels went down and we spent less time going over what we should have said, if only we'd thought of it at the time. People tell us that we're nicer people to deal with too, so they approach us with a more open and constructive attitude. And all this from a little reflection and self-learning that cost virtually nothing.

It very soon dawned on us that assertiveness is a topic of vital importance to everyone in any situation – in particular to managers at all levels working under pressure to maintain progress in organisations. Given that it means taking account of other people's viewpoints, while freeing you to say honestly what you know, think or feel, without offending or threatening others, it has enormous potential for removing blockages and frustrations at work.

Perhaps the central point is that assertiveness is not about winning and losing. It's only about winning. True assertive behaviour helps everyone to win something, as it removes unhealthy competition, the need for one party to beat another. If you win, they win too. It is possible, with solutions to difficult situations that recognise everyone's needs and wants, and that aim for a constructive compromise that gives everyone something.

Most of us have at some stage lived in fear of speaking out, in case someone else thinks we're being awkward, unhelpful or antagonistic. At other times, there are occasions when we need to calm down someone who is angry or aggressive, without losing self-control. Assertiveness helps in both these situations.

Similarly, even though we may not see ourselves as aggressive or intimidating, it can look that way to other people. The way we speak, act and talk conveys messages that may push others back into their shells, or may get their backs up and make them aggressive in return. Assertiveness is not the same as aggression – that's one common misconception to lose from the start – and aggressive people can benefit enormously from a focus on facts and feelings, rather than an approach of thud and blunder.

So we wrote this book, our third in this series. We tried very hard to write it in a way that makes the words come to life, so you can relate the key issues and techniques to your own experience and your own life. We felt that if the book were to make a real difference, that it had to touch nerves and provide situations and experiences that you have had. It is for this reason that we have added to each section what we see as a *Window on the World* of assertiveness.

We have interviewed a selection of managers, one for each chapter, and include a short first-hand testimony of what assertiveness has, and in one case hasn't, done for them. The managers work in a range of different organisations. You will find these windows on assertiveness at the end of each chapter. By the end of the book you will probably be able to add the odd window yourself.

But this approach to writing hasn't been adopted just to give you a good read. You can try out what it says. A theoretical explanation of assertiveness could leave you feeling that it's all a bit vague, a little difficult, and put you off from ever getting started. We're back to where we began this introduction – that's how we felt. Our aim is to open the window on assertiveness, so you experience its power for yourself.

Once you've begun, there's no doubt that you'll continue. Success breeds success. But it's taking the first steps that is often hardest. Give it a try – there's nothing to lose and we really believe that you will become as committed as we are, to a way of communicating that gives you more of what you want without having to beat down other people.

Try it – aim for winning situations all round.

1

The background to assertiveness

High-tech world: low-tech problems

Despite the fact we live in an increasingly high-tech world, the really thorny problems that managers face at work are not generally about computers, software and new technology. The problems that worry and cause stress in most managers are of the distressingly low-tech variety. They are predictable because they are, rather sadly, age-old. That's because people have been around longer than machines, and the problems tend to come from handling people rather than running machinery.

You can sit managers in front of a state-of-the art computer, you can give them a modem and access to the Internet, and they'll find a way of tackling it. The problem is technical, factual and one where there are right and wrong answers, most of the time.

But ask them to handle an awkward confrontation at work, stand up to a disruptive colleague, deal with an angry customer or say simply say 'No' – even when it is perfectly justifiable – and all the computer power in the world won't help.

The chances are if you ask people which sort of problem they would rather have, most will plump for a machine problem.

People are not so predictable or programmable … and you can't just switch them off.

Nevertheless, every human being has to deal with difficult people and situations every day and a manager has to handle people as part of his or her routine. This often means handling conflict and making sense out of turmoil and no matter how many problems you've solved, another thornier version is waiting around the corner.

What assertiveness is and how it helps

■ ■ ■

Assertiveness appears in the book's title, and is our main theme. Naturally, we look in detail at what it means in practice throughout the book, but a basic explanation at this stage is necessary – so you know that we are talking about the same thing. This is especially important because many people confuse assertiveness with aggression. They are not the same thing. Aggressive behaviour is about winning. That inevitably means someone else loses and often the apparent winner loses out in the long term as well.

Assertiveness is about reasonable behaviour that holds your own ground and finds reasonable working compromises, so there are no losers. It's about both sides winning at least something.

Without going into too much detail at this stage, let's agree that:

- some people give in too easily and will do anything to avoid conflict – even agreeing to the impossible;
- other people can be overbearing and aggressive and lead others to agree to things that are either wrong, or unachievable.

Assertive behaviour reduces the negative aspects of both these types. It gives you the right to say what you think and feel calmly and clearly, without giving offence and denying the rights of others to have different views or expectations. You could describe it as being about what you say ... and especially about how you say it.

Machines do what you expect. Learn how to use them and you're in control. But people are different, so shut down your computer, turn off the modem and let high tech have a short break. Start thinking about behaviour and how some simple changes to what you do can bring you better results.

The unpredictability factor

The trouble is that people are emotional and that can make them act or react very awkwardly. The results of this emotion show up when we realise people are:

- often unpredictable, behaving in ways we didn't expect,
- sometimes unreasonable,
- occasionally aggressive,
- surprisingly vulnerable,
- often generous in spirit,
- capable of intuition and compassion,
- liable to have their own firm views about things,
- apt to try to put pressure on you to do what you don't want to do,
- given to clamming up or even saying they are happy about something when they really aren't,
- able to bottle up their anger.

And that's not only the rest of the world, it includes you because you're a human, too. The chances are that from time to time you could recognise yourself in all the statements in the list above. What really matters is how situations go when the pressure is on – and how you feel afterwards.

The acid test

■ ■ ■

The acid test is often the way a difficult person or situation makes you feel afterwards – not just as a result of what they did or said, but more as a result of how you feel you performed.

Self-test 1.1

I WISH ...

Think about a simple situation – say, one where you have been standing in a queue and someone cuts in ahead of you.

The chances are that you either say nothing and steam quietly away inside, or you get angry and a row starts.

Afterwards, you spend hours – the rest of the day sometimes – with the incident running round and round your head. You then probably wish you'd done it differently, either saying something or saying less. But by then it's too late.

It's a common reaction to feel that instead of you having handled a situation, it handled you and you just played a non-speaking walk-on part.

Working in the hot-house

■ ■ ■

The queue-jumping sort of situation is bad enough when you are acting as a private individual, with no one to account for but yourself. But the pressurised environment of organisations tends to act as a kind of greenhouse. Not only do you have to deal with the foibles of *people*, you have to do so in an *environment* and one that makes behaving in a grown-up balanced way difficult.

If all the text-book stuff on ideal organisations were really there, on the ground, it might be different, but there are very few paragons of organisational virtue, where everyone respects each other, cares about colleagues' feelings, works together as a real team or communicates 100 per cent effectively. In most organisations you will see at least some evidence that they are:

- riddled with spoken and unspoken power relationships – between bosses and staff,
- often split with inter-departmental feuds, assumptions and rivalries,
- full of people covering their backs, often at the expense of other parts of the organisation,
- places where people feel increasingly insecure because of the superhuman pace of change.

These are all aspects of organisational culture – which we can define simply as 'the way things are done'. In other words, any organisation will have developed its own character over time, and there is a way of behaving that is seen as normal and acceptable. If the general approach of managers, starting at the top, is to treat people like dirt, to threaten to sack them at the first sign of the slightest problem, and to operate through confrontation and fear, then that's what the organisation is like. That approach becomes normal behaviour and is how staff behave to each other. Anything different just doesn't fit.

So a new member of staff will start to adopt that sort of behaviour as normal ... because that's the way things are done. It's like going to Spain and finding they take a siesta in the afternoon. Before long you adapt the way you operate, so that you take account of that (and other) elements in the local culture. It's easier and it helps you fit in.

The list of cultural aspects – power relationships, rivalries and so on – are ingredients in a recipe for disaster. Fitting in with this culture, where conflict is seen as normal behaviour, makes life a great deal more difficult for you as an individual. If you work in an environment that has even one or two of these or similar factors at work, anything you can do to handle every difficult situation and every potential conflict effectively has got to be for the good.

The organisation and you

■ ■ ■

Assertiveness is a personal philosophy, so it is about you and the way you behave. But you can't divorce that from the context of where you work, so it is also inevitably about your organisation. Some organisations seem to do every darned thing to make it difficult for you to behave in a fruitful, productive, empowered and generally grown-up way. Some simply crush the life and spirit out of people and put so many barriers in your way it would be hard to be assertive (but not impossible) if you wanted to be.

Others seem determined to empower you and help you respond to situations and people in a way that helps – helps you, helps them and helps your organisation.

We'll look at some dreams about what things might be like in an ideal world. Then we'll look at a nightmare, and the reality most managers face before we examine some typical problems and the reactions they provoke.

Personal development

■ ■ ■

If everyone at work operated assertively, the number of problems would drop through the floor. But they don't and you can't expect everyone to change the way they behave, overnight.

The only thing you can change is yourself. Of course, you can help other people to learn what you have learnt, but it has to start with you and you have to be convinced that behaving assertively does pay off. Otherwise you won't bother yourself, let alone try and persuade anyone else about it. What you are likely to find is that once you start making even minor changes to your behaviour, so you act more assertively, other people begin to ask you what your secret is – and that's a good time to share it with them.

Your behaviour and the way you operate can have an impact on the whole organisation – good practice can spread. So there is nothing wrong with accepting you can't change the whole world at once, but need to start with yourself.

For any development, any change in the way someone manages themselves or other people, there have to be three things in place:

- an aim, a picture of what it could and should look like once things have improved,
- a clear picture of where things stand now, so the size and scale of the development needed is clear,
- a strategy for getting from here to there, broken down into achievable steps that help you to build success on success, and make the journey as straightforward as possible.

This chapter will help you to clarify the first two points out of the three, and especially to work out for yourself where you are now and what things are actually like for you where you work. It also introduces some important ideas about why things are like that – how people behave and why difficult situations are difficult.

So let's look at organisations and then move onto some important diagnostic tools you can use to get you started.

We'll start with two fundamentally different caricatures of organisations, called Hades Incorporated and Nirvana Corporation. Each of these – and any other organisation you find – employs three broad types of character. You may recognise these are people whose natural tendency is to operate in the following ways, either as:

- quiet, compliant people who hate any conflict and tend to say 'Yes' rather than cause an upset (even when they really know the answer should be 'No'),

- aggressive individuals who operate by dominating other people, through gruffness, directness and anger that sometimes verges on bullying,
- people who never say much to your face, but whose devious, behind-the-scenes plotting means they invariably get their own way.

Think about the people who spring to mind as you read these descriptions and identify for yourself how you feel about working with them. Then concentrate on identifying some changes that would make things better when you do deal with them – not changes in their behaviour but changes you could make in yours, so you handle them more effectively. By the time you've finished the book you should be in a position to make progress in these areas.

In practice, finding someone who acts purely in one these stereotypical roles is rare – we tend to be a mixture of two or more, depending on the circumstances. But the chances are you know which ones you are most like.

Our two organisations operate in different ways, affecting the strength with which these people's natural tendencies come to the surface.

The manager's day at Hades Incorporated

■ ■ ■

Working at Hades Incorporated may remind you of the worst places you have ever worked in.

You arrive at work at 8 a.m. You're an hour early but the boss yells at you that you're slacking. He's been in since seven.

By 9 o'clock a stack of problems has been dumped on your desk – your secretary is demanding a pay rise or she'll quit; the Midlands office wants a fifty-page report on yesterday's meeting by lunchtime but won't provide the data you need for this morning's directors' meeting; and to cap it all, some joker has stuck a mock league table on the wall, pointing out that his team has made double the number of sales your team has .... so there!

Situations like this make most of us want to scream. Many people, however, buckle under, feeling they have to accept such working circumstances. Generally, the result is a demoralised, fragmented and disorganised workforce, where scoring points off other people is the name of the game and the natural tendencies of our three types of people flourish. The timid people get so overpowered and passive that they feel genuinely ill with stress, the aggressive group give full rein to their ability to bully and the devious bunch have a field day!

We hope you don't work at an organisation like Hades Incorporated, but if you do read on.

Life at Nirvana Corporation

What would it be like working for the ideal organisation? Go on, try to imagine it – the place that you dream of, where you really look forward to going to work, and feel disappointed when the day comes to an end. Maybe your perfect organisation is a bit like the following.

At Nirvana Corporation all the staff communicate clearly. There are never any misunderstandings. No one is aggressive or starts rows. Everyone is supportive and has an optimistic, cheerful outlook on their life at work. Hassles and problems don't exist. Instead there are just challenges and solutions – opportunities that can benefit everyone.

In the ideal organisation people respect each other. They listen to each other. Bullying is banned and people make the effort to understand what you are like.

The office has a positive culture of teamwork, all pulling together to help each other do the best job possible. Even the departments and sections that work in different functions see each other as part of the same overall team, working to solve each others' problems rather than blame the people down the corridor.

Feedback is open and constructive – and shop floor workers are just as happy to tell managers what's good about the way they operate and what changes could make things even better.

Everyone's ideas count

Every employee, manager or shop floor worker has a part to play in the success of Nirvana Corporation. Open communication is encouraged. There are suggestion boxes in every office and ideas are discussed at regular staff meetings. Feedback between managers and their team is a free-flowing, two-way process.

The result is that opportunities are never missed. The directors at Nirvana realise that you can never tell where the next great money-spinning (or time-saving) idea is going to come from.

Case study 1.1

STICKING IT TO THE BOSS

It happens in the real world too. Perhaps one of the best known stories about successful staff innovation surrounds the invention of the *Post-it* note.

3M runs a staff incentive programme to boost new product development. Research staff are encouraged to spend up to 15 per cent of their time researching their own pet projects. The hope is that this will produce a constant stream of new ideas and products.

One scientist, working on adhesive formulas, couldn't get a particular glue to stick properly. Days later, he could still peel one material away from the other. Surely a useless invention – but what about those telephone messages that kept falling behind the desk? The *Post-it* note was born. Without 3M's investment in its staff's ideas, we might still be scrabbling under the desk for that vital lost message!

You don't have to be a specialist to have a good idea, as Kodak found out.

Case study 1.2

A SPLASHING IDEA

Kodak's *depth imaging* is a way of digitally manipulating photos to show scenes in 3-D. Printed on laminated plastic, the image appears to move as the viewer moves his head. You can create video-like sequences, see the inside and outside of a product in one photo, the possibilities are endless.

The initial idea came from one of Kodak's secretaries. On a trip to Disney World, she thought how wonderful it would be to capture all the drama of her son sliding down Splash Mountain, a gigantic water shoot, on one photo. Not just a video film, but a photo that allowed you to get right inside the scene and feel what it was like. Jokingly, she mentioned it to her boss.

He told the development team who said 'Sure, we could do that'. The product is now worth over $235 million to Kodak.

Things aren't working so let's fix them

Employees at Nirvana Corporation are encouraged to say if something is going wrong. No one starts looking for a scapegoat. Saying something's wrong is not destructive whinging, it's constructive feedback. Only when they know here's room for improvement can the company can find a way to fix the problem quickly. Alternatively, if someone is worrying needlessly, they can reassure the employee that things are all right and clearly explain why.

Team work

Staff at Nirvana Corporation see themselves as one big team. They all pull together to achieve a common goal and keep the company successful.

No matter what problems they face, managers and their teams overcome difficulties by compromising to achieve the best possible result for all concerned. Saying 'No', if you really haven't got the time to do something, is fine, so long as another solution is found (including the possibility that the job *can* wait until tomorrow).

Teamwork isn't only about all pulling together. It's about knowing whether or not you are doing a good job and doing it even better the next time.

Above all, staff are encouraged to use and develop their skills and personal styles to the benefit of all. Whatever someone's approach, the company gets the best from them. To do this the organisation has put in place strategies that help and support different types of people.

The culture at Nirvana Corporation means that each of our three types of person curbs the excesses in their personal style and feels it is OK to operate differently. So:

- the passive people feel supported and valued, feel entitled to say what they really feel, but can get on in backroom jobs without feeling pressurised if that's what they do best;
- the aggressive people feel that it is normal in this organisation to listen to people's feelings, using their boundless energy to motivate others in the team;
- the manipulative individuals find it largely unnecessary to plot and connive, and instead convert the energy they would otherwise spend getting their own way into planning with others, rather than against them.

Staff do the best job they are capable of, the company runs smoothly and achieves more due to harmony in the workplace. Above all it is an organisation where you can be yourself and others can be themselves.

Wouldn't this be bliss? It's certainly the other end of the spectrum from Hades Incorporated, the dreaded bastion of all things unempowered and guaranteed to test your assertiveness skills to the limit. It's very unlikely that you work in either – but unfortunately experience tells us that you may have spotted more similarities with Hades than with Nirvana.

Moving on ...

■ ■ ■

So where you work at present, the culture of the place, the way you do things, have a bearing on where it is that you are starting from in your journey towards a more assertive approach.

If you work in a difficult Hades-type organisation then maybe you have further to travel. On the other hand, if you work in an organisation like the following, then the ground will at least be a little more fertile.

Case study 1.3

ALL TOGETHER NOW

Rufus Leonard Design Consultants is a successful design agency with a refreshing approach to management.

There is only one layer of management in the company. All the managers make great efforts to ensure they too are considered part of the team and that everyone in the company is happy to talk to them openly. There are meeting rooms but everyone works in the same space – office doors are left open unless an important meeting is in progress.

The team approach is particularly important when it comes to projects. At Rufus Leonard project teams review how things went at the end of every job. It helps to step back and look at what could be done better the next time around; but that's only half the story. Rufus Leonard also reviews how well the team has worked together. Everyone's opinion counts. The important thing is to improve the group's future performance.

So organisations are important. They are the backdrop to assertiveness. The key is to develop your assertiveness skills wherever you are. It is important though not to get too hung up on looking at organisations.

Sure, some organisations make it difficult to be assertive, others actively encourage it. But assertiveness is essentially about *you*, wherever you work. It is about changing the way you respond to others and to a range of different situations.

The problems experienced by the manager at Hades Incorporated are common – we've all faced similar situations in our day-to-day working lives. No one listens to our opinion; problems don't get solved, they clog up the system; departments work against each other, not as a team and so on. And us, well we curl up and die, or bottle up our feelings of frustration or we just get plain mad.

The great thing about assertive behaviour is that it can help in every situation, not only in Hades. It can make life even better if things are already pretty good.

Working in the real world

■ ■ ■

You live in the real world and have to deal with your own situation, not our stereotypes, so it's time to do some diagnosing.

The following model will help you position yourself, to find out where you are now and why you might be having problems. The aim of the model is to help you to uncover some of your own problems and to understand the kind of areas that can produce conflict and difficulties.

The principle is simple. Too many people wander through their working lives without reflecting on what happens. One idea underpinning this whole book is that we need to, as Baden-Powell might have said, **be prepared** – to think through where problems occur and plan a response. This isn't the same as being on guard, by the way, which implies being closed and defensive.

Diagnostic tool 1.1

ASK SOME SIMPLE QUESTIONS ABOUT YOURSELF

Asking questions is a useful first move. Try to answer the following questions honestly.

Where are you now?

1 In the past week what were the situations you either didn't handle properly, or you feel you could have handled better?

2 How many were there and what specifically went wrong in a couple of the most memorable?

3 Thinking of the incidents, how much do you think was down to you and how much down to the company?

4 Who was involved in the incidents?

5 What, ideally, would you have done differently?

Asking simple questions about the way the world is for you at the moment can start you thinking through where your flash-points and difficulties are occurring. This activity will also give you some concrete things to work on as you make your way through this book.

This kind of activity can also help you to start to see patterns and common threads. If:

- you uncovered that you have lots of different, difficult and unsatisfactory incidents each week, then you clearly need to start tackling the problems quickly;
- you found only a few incidents but they were all of a similar kind, then this activity will give you a more pinpointed view of areas you need to work on;
- you couldn't think of any problem incidents, then there are a few possible reasons:

1 You are covering up because you don't want to admit, even to yourself, that any such situations arose; if this is the case and you know it in your heart, you need to come to terms with the fact that the only person who loses out if you deny reality is you.

2 You are naturally someone who is aggressive and doesn't realise the effect you have on other people; they may have been really badly affected by a situation that you didn't even spot.

3 You are already very skilled in handling people and situation assertively; in that case you will still find that some of the ideas in the book will help you hone your skills.

4 You are a hermit, with no human contact.

If you found question five in *Where are you now?* hard to answer, take heart. So do most people at this stage.

Diagnostic tool 1.2

IDENTIFY SOME TYPICAL STICKING POINTS

The next step is to be clear about some very common sticking points where people often find it difficult to handle the situation effectively. You'll see they are almost pathetically straightforward and mundane. It is the small stuff, the common things that often trip us up.

Try the following activity.

How you would react to the following problems?

It's 4 p.m. Marketing want all the detail on your new product by tomorrow morning for their hottest client. Do you:

1 Say 'Yes' and beaver away all night to get the job there on time? ❐

2 Say 'No' but arrange to deliver the goods in a couple of days? ❐

Your bump into your best client at a trade fair – and he's talking to your arch-rival in your company, Fred Bloggs. There's this tricky technical question Fred can't answer, but then again you're not sure either. Do you:

1 Answer it anyway – if anything's wrong you can update him tomorrow and anyway it will be his problem by then? ❐

2 Say you don't know. Promise to get back to him tomorrow (then get your technical team to fax the answer *urgently*)? ❐

Gina and Alex storm into your office. Alex has just got a pay rise and Gina can't believe she's been passed over. Once they've calmed down do you:

1 Tell Gina it's OK, she's got a pay rise too even though you weren't planning to give her one – you were going to tell her in your 1:1 this afternoon? ❐

2 Make it plain this isn't the time or place to discuss the issue. Insist they apologise and get back to work. You'll talk to them, individually, later? ❐

You're running a team brainstorm. Jack has a good idea but, as usual, Tom keeps interrupting and saying it's stupid. Do you:

1 Get tough – tell Tom to shut up or get out and show him up in front of the others, as he does with other people? ❐

2 Remind Tom he'll have the chance to comment later, and ask Jack to continue (making a mental note to sit down and talk to Tom privately about the way he behaves)? ❐

Most managers will recognise at least some of these situations. All cause on-going problems for people at work and in life. Generally, the more you said that the first answers were like you, the greater the problem you may have. These tend to be either aggressive or passive answers.

The situations are all about how difficult it can be to say no and how tempting it is to always want to be liked and how difficult it is to hurt someone's feelings ...

All are problematic and to many represent early examples of 'do not pass go'. The second answer to each of the problems above was the more assertive, and effective, way of handling things. But turning the theory into practice is where this book comes in.

Understanding why and how these situations can cause problems goes a long way towards learning how to overcome them.

Do this, you can avoid the pitfalls and learn to make the most of adverse situations. The really crucial point here is that while 'Yes' is a fine word, sometimes 'No' is better.

Saying 'No'

Most people like to be helpful and lend a hand. It's not always possible to be the Good Samaritan but saying 'No' can be extremely hard. However, breaking through the compulsion to say 'Yes' can be seen as the starting gate for any attempt to be more assertive. In many ways it is the royal road to assertiveness.

Have at look at these examples. The first shows the dangers of always saying 'Yes' – and being too forceful with requests. The second is about a missed opportunity to nip conflict in the bud.

Case study 1.4

TOO MUCH TO DO, NOT ENOUGH TIME

Recently a hospital porter found himself confronted by a request he thought he couldn't refuse when he delivered some equipment to theatre.

The surgeon was doing a hip replacement and needed an extra pair of hands. Of course, the porter could help. It was against hospital regulations for untrained staff to assist during operations. The porter knew he could lose his job but the surgeon insisted – very loudly. What could he say?

Although the operation was a success, the national press got hold of the story and a scandal ensued. The porter and surgeon were disciplined. For months to come staff had to reassure terrified patients that they wouldn't be operated on by a porter.

Case study 1.5

IT'LL BE THERE IN THE MORNING ... PROMISE

A supervisor in a builder's merchant who took a telephone order agreed under pressure from the customer to deliver the goods by 10 a.m. the next day. When the customer rang at 2.30 to find out what was going on, and to let the builder know because there was a gang of workers standing around waiting, the answer came back that it certainly wouldn't be today. The lorry was in for servicing and had been booked in for over three weeks ... everyone knew that.

Ever been in a similar situation? Sadly, it's probably a silly question.

Most of these problems arise when the person asking is told what they want to hear rather than the truth. 'Yes' instead of 'No, but maybe we could do it this way'. It may mean facing an initial conflict but the end result is far less damaging and traumatic. Trying to please everyone is a short route to disaster – and high blood pressure! We'll look at how to handle these situations assertively and win through later it the book.

'No' may be one of the shortest words in the dictionary, but it can feel like one of the hardest to use.

Diagnostic tool 1.3

UNDERSTANDING WHERE CONFLICT HAPPENS

So the word 'Yes' can be a real sticking point. But use it and it can get you into all sorts of trouble. Now let's look at some other common areas where conflict occurs.

The obvious and hidden sources of conflict

An important skill that all front-line managers need is the ability to identify problems and conflict, preferably before they arise. It's unlikely you'll ever be prepared for every crisis but, unlike the lottery numbers, you don't need to be Mystic Meg to predict where some problems will come from.

There are a number of places you can look – some of them are patently obvious, others can be pretty unexpected.

The following is a list for starters. All the following can trigger conflict.

- racism,
- sexism,
- differences of opinion,
- distressing personal habits – anything from clearing the throat to constant wisecracking,
- not fitting in with the way things are normally done in the organisation – in some places seemingly innocuous behaviour can cause real conflict,
- any other discriminatory behaviour,
- poor communications,
- working conditions,
- unrealistic expectations of what is possible.

The obvious places where conflict occurs

■ ■ ■

One of the most obvious places is where relations are already strained and personalities clash. Sometimes people just cannot get on together, for no logical reason. As a manager you have to decide whether to evade conflict (by separating the individuals concerned) or avoid it (e.g. set ground rules to ensure they work constructively together).

Another obvious source of conflict is when your team are under pressure and understaffed. When people work long hours under extreme pressure tempers tend to snap.

Overt conflict can have a dreadful effect on morale. Very few people honestly enjoy full-blown slanging matches. When bickering and arguments become a regular part of the office day it is important to tackle the problem quickly.

The less obvious places

■ ■ ■

Managers also need to be aware of the covert sources of conflict lurking within their department. The hidden incendiary device waiting to explode without warning.

Covert conflict, by nature, can be difficult to detect. This makes it particularly damaging for anyone who is unaware that it exists – new employees, other departments, colleagues or customers, etc. Whilst everything looks calm on the surface, this ticking time bomb can undermine your position and your team's performance.

What causes covert conflict? A long-standing team member being passed over for promotion. A team member who constantly sniffs or wears strange clothes. The reasons needn't be terribly logical!

Ask yourself where at work have you seen overt and covert conflict? Think of some examples – ones that you've experienced personally or perhaps witnessed:

- examples of overt conflict,
- examples of covert conflict.

Everyone's personal experience will be different. However, this activity should help you to think analytically about the kinds of conflicts you may need to manage as a front-line manager.

It is worth remembering that overt conflicts are hard to ignore. Managers need to be seen to solve these problems swiftly. Covert conflicts, on the other hand, are all to easy to sweep under the carpet in the hopes they will disappear. Mostly they just fester and get harder to solve in the long run.

The following are some of the key flash point areas that need to be managed:

- people feeling they do not have the chance to discuss their problems,
- misunderstandings about the standard of work expected, or the way changes had been introduced,
- a breakdown in trust, for instance where something you are told in confidence becomes common knowledge because you let it slip to someone else,
- small irritations are not identified and dealt with quickly.

Diagnostic tool 1.4

UNDERSTAND YOUR OWN ATTITUDES TO DIFFICULT SITUATIONS

This will give you a clearer picture of why you respond in the way you do now and how you can start to alter your response in the future.

Our reactions to difficult situations can be complex. Most of us gain experience of conflict from watching the world around us, teenage rows with our parents, our own mistakes – a muddled assortment of experience that can relay very confused messages. Let's look at some of the typical reactions to conflict or potential conflict.

Fear of being disliked

The desire to avoid conflict by any means possible is often rooted in a fear of being disliked. How often do we want to complain but hold back to avoid causing any ill feeling? Your hairdresser is transforming you into a Bart Simpson look-alike, but he'll be hurt if you say something. So you sit and suffer the indignity in silence.

The desire to be liked – or rather the fear of being disliked – is hugely important. It leads us to say 'Yes' when we mean 'No', so the other person likes us in the short term. But what happens when we don't deliver? They dislike us – and lose respect for us – far more than if we'd stood our ground in the first place.

Complaining about work colleagues is even harder. You need to work with them in future. Maybe they're friends as well as colleagues. However, avoiding criticism in case it causes offence can be foolhardy. You can ignore the problem but it is unlikely to go away.

It's worth remembering two points. Telling someone you disagree with them can be difficult. After all, the word criticism tends to have negative connotations for most people. Managers who convey such views as constructive feedback generally receive a better hearing. We'll look at how to provide constructive feedback later in the book.

Also remember that it's important to believe in yourself. Everyone is entitled to an opinion. The ability to debate different ideas and reach a consensus is a key skill for today's front-line manager. To adapt a phrase from the *Financial Times*, 'No comment, no opinion'.

Fight or flight

Cavemen knew a thing or two about conflict. Faced with a slavering sabre-toothed tiger they had two options – beat it over the head with a club or sprint up the nearest tree. These instinctive reactions are still strong and are characterised by a rush of adrenaline that brings blood to our muscles and nerve ends.

You'll have experienced that, under any sort of stress the palms of your hands get a bit clammy, the heart races, you sweat a bit and you seem keyed up. What stresses one person may not affect another, of course, but maybe you'll recognise the symptoms from when you have to address a large audience and you're waiting in the wings, or you are due to go in for a job interview, or a really angry customer starts insulting you without any preamble. The way your body reacts is the genetic hangover from when you may have met a sabre-toothed tiger and had just the two options of running or fighting. What happens is your brain recognises the threat and triggers the adrenaline rush to tell your body there's a threat about and set it up for peak performance, whether it's fight or flight.

All twentieth-century human beings have done is adapt this automatic reaction to today's environment.

Case study 1.6

THE COURT JESTER

British Airways have developed a novel approach which enables them to air criticism whilst avoiding potential conflict between colleagues.

Board meetings at BA nowadays are a bit of a laugh. Realising that directors were loathe to criticise each other in front of all their colleagues, BA hired an outsider to do it for them.

Now, a court jester attends certain board meetings to poke fun at everyone in the room. Some of the jests are stupid and outrageous; others may have a ring of truth about them – but still make everyone laugh.

The aim is to help get tricky issues out into the open without getting too personal. Everyone receives the same treatment, no one feels they are being singled out – and laughing about their shortcomings helps the directors see the funny side and realise that maybe it's not such a hard problem to deal with after all.

Taking flight

It is rarely appropriate to run away from conflict, certainly not in a management role. So, the desire to escape turns into a demonstration of submission, a form of passive behaviour. However, the emotional aftermath of submitting is that you feel guilty, and believe that you have let yourself down.

Passive behaviour that belies the desire to flee can take some of or all of the following forms:

- withdrawn eye contact,
- withdrawn body language, hiding, looking smaller,
- words – continual apologies and agreement.

This passive approach generally creates more problems than it solves. It also makes future conflict more, rather than less likely, for the passive manager who flees from conflict gets known as an easy target.

Fight

■ ■ ■

The other instinctive option is to fight. Most people hold short of flattening the opposition but still behave aggressively. It is the common belief that one has to fight fire with fire, to strike first to avoid defeat.

Aggressive behaviour is equally unsatisfactory and has its own tell-tale signs:

- vocal – raised, clipped or sarcastic tone of voice,
- the wagging finger, the clenched fist, or banging the table and waving the arms,
- staring and invasive eye contact,
- oppressive body language – standing too close, bearing down on the target,
- not listening, interrupting or permitting a response.

Everyone has experienced the natural desire to fight or flee at some stage in their working lives. Assertiveness is not natural. It is acquired and developed, but once mastered it will help you to handle conflict so that everyone wins.

Diagnostic tool 1.5

DIG DEEPER TO UNDERSTAND CONFLICT

Now it's time to dig a little below the surface. There are other reasons why conflict breaks out that you should be aware of.

Cultural issues

When dealing with a tricky problem it often helps to put yourself in the other person's shoes. Is it possible that they perceive things in an entirely different way from you?

Cultural issues can play a large part here – and some problems can have blindingly simple explanations. A Dutch businessman may be irritated that you can't despatch his goods on May 1st. Does he know it's a public holiday? Or the secretary who is happy to work late whenever she is asked – but why won't she stay on a Friday? Maybe she's Jewish and has to get home before sundown.

Other difficulties can be harder to identify, rooted in the general cultural approach to life and work.

Gender issues

Regrettably, sexual discrimination is a real problem in the workplace today. It is an issue which needs to be taken seriously and handled sensitively. The law surrounding allegations of sexual discrimination is complex. Managers who find themselves confronted by this problem should seek professional advice through their human resources department.

There are many other, less obvious conflicts which may be linked to issues of gender. Many women managers believe they have experienced the glass ceiling syndrome. They fail to gain promotion, despite a superb track record within their organisation, and can find no reason why. Regardless of whether or not this very real problem exists in your organisation, it is as well for managers to be aware of this fear.

Some male employees may have problems handling what they see as role reversal (working for a woman). The usual doubts about challenging your boss or capitulating get magnified – if you disagree are you an obstreperous arrogant man and a male chauvinist pig? Agree and will people – especially other 'macho' male managers – think you're a weak-willed wimp?

Everyone in your team will have their own perspective on these issues. It is important as a manager to make sure you know what their point of view is and whether it is likely to cause any friction in the workplace. An assertive approach to talking and listening can help you to tease this information out.

Case study 1.7

NICHT GEGEN DIE ORDNUNG

Ford, the US car manufacturing giant, run their European headquarters from Cologne in Germany. The manufacturing plant is highly productive, the head office atmosphere positive and everybody gets their job done.

Management at Ford came up against an unexpected problem. Although hard workers, few German managers seemed keen to act on their initiative, to do more than the specific job they were employed to do. So American and UK managers were often drafted in to Cologne to reorganise or develop departments.

Inadvertently, this is helping to solve the problem. It's common for German middle managers to have PhDs and MBAs, so there was no shortage of talent. What they weren't used to was the idea that rules (die Ordnung) could be flexible, job descriptions could be guidelines for adaptation (where appropriate) rather than regulations to be followed verbatim. Working with overseas colleagues in Germany and abroad, Ford's managers are learning to understand the way other countries think, and learning to use each other's strengths to the company's advantage.

Diagnostic tool 1.6

DO THE TALKING AND LISTENING TEST

And finally it is important to think about talking and listening. All too often conflicts break out because communication breaks down.

It's good to talk

As we've seen, failure to communicate clearly is one of the simplest, and unfortunately commonest, causes of conflict in organisations. Perhaps modern technology can provide the solution?

In all honesty, it probably can't. The computer age has spawned an enormous range of gadgets via which people can communicate with each other. Modems, video coms, satellite links and so on are all marvellous ways of enhancing communication – but none of them should be seen as a replacement for good personal, face-to-face communication.

It is all too easy to get cut off from reality. Unless you have an acute sixth sense or a degree in psychology, it is difficult to tell what people are really thinking if your only method of communication is the phone, fax or e-mail. Bob Hoskins may tell us that its 'good to talk' but it's important to listen and watch as well.

You can do a quick test about whether you are a good listener (which incidentally is another part of the royal road to assertiveness).

Do you:

- find that you interrupt people when they are speaking to you?
- get impatient and finish sentences for them?
- switch off while listening?
- look bored?

Answer 'Yes' and you come lower in the listening stakes than Bob Maxwell. And why is listening so important? Well, for starters if you don't listen then you aren't showing respect for the person who is talking, and without respect there can be no assertiveness.

Case study 1.8

A CULTURAL EVENING

Serco is an international facilities management company. It manages an extensive range of facilities including airports, leisure centres and parks, high street stores and even ESTEC, HQ of the European Space Agency.

Managed from the UK, Serco's operations are based all over the world – which can make it hard to really keep in touch. So Serco's directors take the time to visit sites and hold what they call 'culture evenings'.

Staff spend a social evening with the director, *without* their boss. They're encouraged to be honest about how things are going, to mention any problems and to say what's good about working in their department. It's easier for the team to give constructive feedback to an independent party and it helps their boss to discuss the issues with the director who understands the bigger picture.

The makings of a better manager

■ ■ ■

That's it for Chapter 1.

You've looked at an ideal vision of organisations and seen how things often work out. You've also worked through a diagnostic model that shows the kind of difficult situations people face.

So how can you, as a manager, go about learning to handle difficult situations effectively – and feel better about the outcome. Assertiveness can play a large part in achieving this. Everyone has the ability to learn to be assertive, without having to change their character radically or do things that are likely to make them feel uncomfortable.

In the rest of this book we will go on to look at the different personal styles of management and how you can adapt these to become an assertive manager. So this book aims to help you to become a better and more effective manager. On a slighter grander scale it aims to help you be more effective outside work as well.

The final element of this, and indeed every, chapter in this book is a window on assertiveness. This first window is provided by a person who runs their own business from home. It shows how they came to understand what assertiveness is and how they use it day-to-day.

Window 1

SO THAT'S WHAT ASSERTIVENESS IS!

Assertive behaviour has really helped me to keep control of the business I run. Although to be honest I didn't realise what it was when I first encountered it!

Several years ago I worked for Cambridgeshire Social Services in the personnel division. It was a busy department, like so many personnel sections, we seemed to wage a constant battle looking to replace people and maintain headcounts. It was very stressful. People tended to lose their tempers a lot. The head of the division was an exception to the rule. He was well known for always getting his own way and winning these battles. I was really impressed the first time I saw him in action – he kept repeating himself, explaining the point he wanted to get across. No matter how long it took he'd just keep plugging away and never lost his temper. And he always kept smiling.

It was a lesson I remembered when I started my own business. Clients tend to want everything urgently. It's all too easy to say 'Yes' just to please them even though you know the deadlines aren't realistic. So I've always made it a rule to be honest about how much work I can take on. Some people don't like it. They get angry because they think I'm being unhelpful ... mainly the men! I just keep smiling and say I'm happy for them to take the work elsewhere but I'd rather be honest about deadlines than disappoint people. In the long run it's worth it because I deliver on time and the client is happy.

In fact, one client eventually admitted as much. He used to bluster and shout to get his own way until one day, mid-flow he burst out laughing. 'It's marvellous Diane, everyone else always gives in but you don't. And you're charming about it too!' Now he never argues with me – he knows I'm just being honest, not obstreperous.

2

■ ■ ■

I'm really sorry, but I hate you

Assertiveness matters

■ ■ ■

We said at the start of the book that assertiveness is the theme. Indeed a large part of it is about the techniques of assertiveness. But assertiveness is about much more than techniques. It is about:

- handling difficult situations more effectively,
- understanding where you are coming from – what situations you can and can't handle at present,
- having a sense of self-worth,
- helping you to control the way you feel about the world and the people in it rather than the other way round,
- recognising your own and other people's rights and responsibilities.

It is generally about being a more effective person. Let's explore that a bit further, by looking first at what it is and is not, and at some ways assertiveness can help you get better results.

What assertiveness means to you

There are many versions of a definition of assertiveness, but we feel it is clearly expressed in this way.

> ***Definition***
>
> ***ASSERTIVENESS***
>
> Handling yourself and your behaviour so you manage situations and deal with people in a confident and self-assured way. Working to reach a satisfactory conclusion for everyone concerned, by listening to their views and honestly and clearly expressing your own views and feelings so they are heard by the other person(s) without being hurtful, destructive or counter-productive.

This needs unpacking a bit. Saying what you feel, think or believe is not the same as shouting someone else down or pulling rank. That's aggression, a very different approach from assertiveness, which means believing you have the right to say your piece calmly, rationally to express your own views while recognising their right to get the same respect from you. Assertiveness has nothing to do with beating the other person, either by bullying them or by devious and underhand means. That implies pleasure in their failure, and that is not a satisfactory conclusion.

Assertiveness affects the way you handle situations and people, and helps you maintain self-control and in control of the situation. It is not about controlling another person, because that would mean you were exercising power over them – an issue that runs directly counter to the assertiveness philosophy. Often, the 'satisfactory conclusion' in assertiveness is a compromise, or even you changing your mind based on facts and information someone else gives you.

This is what one supervisor said about the way an assertive team member helped them get things right.

'I said we had to finish the job by Friday. But Derek said that was impossible, because we had the Stubbings contract to complete first. I'm afraid I lost my rag and said sharply that I wasn't there to argue ... just do it!

'But he said, calmly, that he understood the pressure we were all under and he was concerned as well. He also pointed out again something that I knew, really, but didn't want to face – that it was physically impossible to do both jobs. He just said that he understood, and wanted to make sure the team was successful, but that we couldn't use the same machine on both jobs at once ... so which one should we concentrate on?

'What he was really saying was that nobody can do the impossible, so it's stupid to say we can. Much better to sort out priorities first. I felt very nervous but when I went back to the boss and explained the difficulty I was amazed. She actually thanked me! She phoned Stubbings, asked what was absolutely essential for the weekend and then rescheduled the work. Derek saved me, and all he did was tell me what I already knew.'

So assertiveness does not mean winning all the personal arguments or all the battles. The supervisor in the example might have felt they'd won the battle if Derek had said he'd do his best and had given in, but it wouldn't have changed the real situation. Come the weekend everyone would have lost – customer, boss, supervisor, team. There is absolutely no mileage in seeing every situation as a battle that someone has to win. Not only is it impossible to win every time, but also it follows that if there is a winner there must be a loser ... which could be you next time.

Assertiveness *does* mean you will generally get better results – but not from scoring points off other people and putting them down. Success comes from handling yourself with confidence in the situation you saw in Chapter 1, where someone jumps the queue in front of you. Think a bit more about this queue situation.

If you do a Victor Meldrew, shout at the queue-jumper and get angry, the chances are they will do the same to you. You get stressed and develop a deep sense of frustration that stays with you for hours. You remain angry for the rest of the day.

All right, they may crumble, feel embarrassed and frightened and move to the back – but is that the sort of effect you want to have on people? Do you want this individual to tell their friends what an animal you were, and point you out in the street when they see you?

In a survey on stress carried out by Abbey Life Assurance, the TV characters that the public said were most stressed were Basil Fawlty and Victor Meldrew – both aggressive and angry people.

Or, instead of becoming aggressive, you say nothing so you still get angry and frustrated, but inside – as much with yourself as with them.

And the bottom line is that in neither case are they likely to have moved to the back of the queue! Even if they did, it was at the expense of their – and your – dignity.

So instead of shouting, or saying nothing, you act with great care and tact and express your views and feelings calmly and logically. They still may not move – but there is more chance that way than through the other approaches, so it can produce better instant results. But even if they don't, at least you feel that you said your piece, stayed calm and did not get too stressed. The rest of the day is not ruined.

If you doubt this, think about it from the other end. How do you react if, say, you have parked in a space in a packed car park, without realising someone else had been waiting for it? Suddenly you're confronted by a red-faced and fuming driver who shouts abuse at you and says you stole the place they were waiting for. Do you move? Not likely! Chances are you get angry back … probably shouting your last insult over your shoulder as you walk away, leaving them still with no parking place. Alternatively, you don't even know about the person who sits in their car, livid that you shot into the place they were patiently waiting for – they just drive away muttering behind their car windows.

But what if someone reasonable comes up? What if they say that they realise the car park is busy, and they're sure you hadn't realised they had been waiting for ten minutes for the other car to pull out, so they would really appreciate you moving. You may not move, but the chances are much greater that you will agree to this approach than to being abused and shouted at – in fact you may even apologise as you reverse out.

Assertiveness is not a quick fix

■ ■ ■

There are techniques to be used – and we look at them in some detail in this book. But the fundamental approach to assertiveness is about developing your ability to act with confidence, and that's what the book is really about.

It is true that we all have a history based on our past experiences and that our genetically natural reaction to situations tends to stem from the physical flight or fight reaction. But assertiveness is based on acknowledging these experiences and moving beyond them. It is, therefore, acquired and basically unnatural behaviour, a way of operating that has to be learnt and developed.

Everyone learns the vast majority of what they know, whether it's facts or how to operate with other human beings, from life. We all pick up clues from experiences along life's road and adopt strategies that work for us, bit by bit. We do this so gradually that we don't even notice we're doing it.

This means that everyone has some assertive behaviour which they have developed, and nobody is entirely passive or aggressive. But many people have never even thought about how this happens and what they do, simply because it has been learnt without them noticing.

In case you feel that learning about assertiveness is a 'soft' issue, not for strong people and all a bit trendy, listen to what three middle managers wrote as feedback after they had completed a course of ten sessions, one day a week on basic management skills.

> *'When I saw the programme I could see why delegation, time management and planning were in there, but I groaned when I*

saw one day was on assertiveness. I expected flabby and wishy-washy stuff about equal opportunities and sexism ... and I was wrong. It is probably the session in the course that will make the biggest difference to the way I manage.'

'This ought to be compulsory for all managers. I learnt a lot about myself and how I could do better, especially from the assertiveness session.'

'I had entirely the wrong idea of what assertiveness meant. I thought it was about beating the opposition, so I wasn't looking forward to it because I can do that already! It's quite challenging to find that if I soften my line I can get better results.'

Like that session, the whole topic of assertiveness is about you as a person, and how you interact with all those other mysterious, different and unique persons around you. Nobody else can do it for you.

It is a very powerful fact that no two people operate in exactly the same way – human beings are uniquely different from each other. This helps explain why there can't be a set of rules and techniques that suits everybody universally, unlike the rules that come with a machine or a computer program. It is not just a question of pressing buttons in the right order to get a result – it's about feelings, emotions and communication; yours and theirs.

Understanding your personal style

This book is based on you developing an understanding of the way you work. It is also based on a belief that we need to go beyond the way we work *now* and develop new and more effective and rewarding ways of working.

So one of the first stages is to look at what our preferred personal style is.

It is fair to say that people do often have rather strange ideas about personal styles. These include the view:

- That we are as we are and should simply do what feels natural,
- That how we are is bred in the bone and any attempt to change it is largely a waste of time.

In this chapter we'll stand back and look at some of the different personal styles of handling the difficult business of conflict, what's good and bad about them. We'll also look at assertiveness: what it is (and isn't); how it works; and what it can do for you – enhancing without necessarily changing your personal style. Then you will know what you do already and can identify skills and techniques you want to develop, to become more assertive.

Who am I?

■ ■ ■

It is important to think a little about the way you **are** as well as the way **you** behave. And this involves asking an important **why** question?

Why do I behave in the way I do in certain situations?

In some ways this means looking at the way we have been programmed to behave – at the way the past intrudes on the present. This chapter looks at some simple examples of that programming. So, some people behave aggressively when faced with conflict, others curl up and act passively.

Part off this programming is age-old – the fight-or-flight cave-dweller response to problems which we looked at in the first chapter. But unfortunately our responses to conflict are not just dictated by this rather primeval response.

In short, the way we grow up and our experiences along the way tend to have a great bearing on the way we respond when conflict is in the air. This isn't really a book about psychology and it certainly doesn't aim to be a do-it-yourself guide to psychoanalysis, but it is worth touching on a few areas as preparation.

> ***Definition***
>
> ***TRANSACTIONAL ANALYSIS***
>
> Transactional analysis is a system which analyses people's behaviour. It argues that in any situation we behave in role. This role is dictated by our earlier experiences and possibly even by our genes.
>
> Broadly speaking, transactional analysis says that in given situations we behave either as child or parent. So faced with conflict we may act as a child, running away, throwing a tantrum, engaging in a metaphorical playground scrap, sublimating our own wishes or simply crumpling up. Alternatively our pattern of behaviour may well be that we take the role of assertive adult when facing conflict.
>
> Transactional analysis says that we need to understand the way we behave in order to address it and develop our behaviour patterns.

Whatever approach you look at the basic idea is simple. That people behave in certain unhelpful ways because they haven't learned how to reprogramme that behaviour.

It may sound simplistic but people often respond passively to conflict because they learned when growing up that this seems, at least on the surface, to be the quickest way of getting it over. Conversely, some people behave aggressively, again because they feel that it also gets the difficult business of conflict out of the way quickly and, of course, to their own advantage.

People's upbringing can instil many rather negative attitudes. Many people have a low sense of self-esteem brought on by parents who couldn't, or wouldn't, show approbation or affection. In many ways this rather basic programming affects the way we respond to situations later on.

The truth is, though, that assertiveness can help you to make the most of your personal approach to handling conflict, to get the best results for you and your team.

It is important to say though that this book takes a rather iconoclastic approach. We do believe that assertiveness *usually* will help you to handle conflict more effectively and we explain why in this chapter. But sometimes a good old bout of aggressive, manipulative, or indeed passive, behaviour is what is required. It is all about selecting the right style for the right situation.

In battle, faced with a conflict against a crack troop of heavily armed SAS men, a good dose of passivity (straightforward running away or surrender) is probably by far the best approach.

Reacting to conflict

First, you need to identify, honestly, how you react to conflict. Let's look at some of the natural styles.

A small problem of recognition

As you read about passive and aggressive people, you may start to assume that aggressive individuals don't need any more assertiveness – they are there already and can stand up for themselves pretty well already, thank you very much! Unfortunately, aggressive people often believe this themselves – and that's a real difficulty. However, remember as you read that assertive people are neither passive nor aggressive. This will become clearer as the chapter unfolds.

This serious problem of recognition needs spelling out again very clearly. It is that:

- passive people generally yearn to be more able to speak up and raise their profile, so they recognise they could do better in the assertiveness stakes;
- aggressive people, on the other hand, often fail to recognise their own problem – or the problems they cause through giving other people a hard time; they mistakenly think they win anyway, so they don't need to change.

The problem is that aggressive behaviour distorts situations, leads to further conflict and produces bad results, so aggressive individuals benefit from working towards assertiveness just as much as passive people do. All we ask before going into detail is that you recognise that statement, especially if you (or someone who is brave enough to tell you their opinion) feel you're aggressive. You'll prove it for yourself as you read on.

Passive or submissive?

■ ■ ■

There are probably ten times as many naturally passive people in your office as aggressive ones. Then again, you probably haven't noticed.

The passive people may be the quiet ones who never argue or say boo to a goose. They may be the gregarious ones. They sometimes look as if they haven't a care in the world, always joking and laughing – and underneath it all are insecure and uncomfortable.

Passivity can cause you and the people themselves a whole host of problems.

So what does passive behaviour look like? Well, there are some pretty obvious things. If passive people get into conflict they exhibit:

- withdrawn eye contact, looking down, hiding behind hair,
- withdrawn body language, hiding, looking smaller,
- words, including 'sorry' and continual agreement.

Quite often, passive or submissive people are just as frustrating and difficult to handle as the aggressive ones. They agree to things without question, leaving you in doubt and worried about the results. They give in and then mutter to themselves afterwards, or they never seem to come up with any new ideas or suggestions.

The worse thing is that at the time it can feel as if you are pushing a sponge – there's nothing there to give you any feel of what they really think. Afterwards the worry and anxiety sets in, and you may decide either to get someone else to do it next time or to keep giving extra work to them because they don't cause any initial conflict.

One of the problems with passivity is that people say 'Yes', when they really have no chance of doing what they promised. They don't want to disappoint or get into trouble. This leads to passive people disappointing others and this tends to reinforce the low self-esteem that is so often associated with passive people.

Another problem is making excuses, rather than telling the truth. Examples of this are so common that you can spot them every day, in every situation. Here's one from an evening's television viewing.

Case study 2.1

AS TIME GOES BY

As Time Goes By is a BBC TV situation comedy about a couple, Jean and Lionel, who get together in their middle years and start life together. In an episode in January 1996, they take over Lionel's family home in the country and plan to go there for weekends. On the first weekend they discover there's a 'county set' that seems to live in each other's pockets every weekend. Jean and Lionel realise they are going to be invited to a couple's home for a precious Sunday that they wanted for themselves and they don't want to go.

They debate how to get out of it and come up with strategies ranging from saying Lionel has suddenly developed measles, to telling the truth; 'Thanks, but we really don't want to come'. They decide to tell the truth, but when the phone rings Jean can't do it, and says that Lionel has suddenly come down with measles.

This is not an uncommon situation. But the aftermath of coming up with a lame excuse is potentially much harder to cope with than telling the truth. It may work in the immediate term, but it brings even greater problems later. For instance, the measles will get better, so what do they do then? Or what if their new 'friends' discover it has been a lie?

Another situation that passive people often get into is when they speak in code. They are so scared of upsetting people and so intent on avoiding anything that they tend to skirt round things. This has the effect of making their meaning unclear, or when you know they are talking in code, downright annoying.

The following story was told to us by a person on one of our training courses.

'I realise now that my old dad was a terribly passive person and this probably why he drove me mad. For a start he would never say anything directly. So, once when my wife and I were moving he said: "It's handy for all those buses going into the town centre there isn't it?" What he meant was that he was worried we would be annoyed by the noise of the buses. I was an old hand at reading him and this kind of thing was really annoying. I would much rather he said directly "Those old buses whistle down your road, won't you find them annoying?"

'The other thing he used to do was to do anything to avoid possible trouble or conflict. So if ever anyone in the family was ill he'd always be first on the phone with some homespun wisdom that proved that the illness wasn't serious after all. You see, if it wasn't serious then nothing bad could happen and no conflict or heartache could result. The best example was when I had to have an appendectomy and 15 minutes before he was still saying it was wind!'

Definition

PASSIVE BEHAVIOUR MEANS:

- apologising for own beliefs and being self-effacing,
- not standing up for your own rights, or standing up for them half-heartedly so others can disregard them,
- not being honest about what you want, or feel.

And you?

How do you fit in? Would you say that you are passive when it comes to conflict? Do you tend to back down, or agree to things you shouldn't? If you do think you are passive, don't panic, there are things you can do about it. But what effects does it have on people?

The effects of passive behaviour on individuals

■ ■ ■

Passive behaviour has a number of effects. In the short term it may reduce people's level of anxiety as they avoid conflict.

But because passive people say 'Yes' when they shouldn't they frequently end up taking on too much work, or not delivering on time and the cycle of disappointment and guilt begins all over again.

The initial buzz of avoiding conflict is rapidly replaced by:

- a feeling that you have let yourself down,
- panic about what you have agreed to do,
- even lower self-esteem.

If you look at the effects on other people you may well see that they are starting to show a lack of respect for you. This is because they don't know what you stand for, or maybe they doubt your integrity as a result of your passive behaviour. They may initially express their feelings by feeling sorry for you. But eventually they will start to feel irritated and cease to respect you.

In the extreme, passive behaviour can make people ill as their confidence plummets and a cycle of guilt sets in.

The effects of passive behaviour on the organisation

■ ■ ■

The effects on an organisation are particularly damaging if you behave passively. Conflicts won't be handled properly and they may break out again at a later date. Difficult decisions may be avoided or delayed and this will affect the outcomes of a team's work. The trouble is that, as you saw when you looked at some positive sides to conflict, giving in temporarily may just mean that you are in for even more conflict later.

Sometimes avoiding conflict *may* be the correct approach.

This checklist covers the key times when it is best to try to avoid conflict.

Checklist 2.1

IT'S BEST TO SAY NOTHING AT THE TIME WHEN ...

- It's the wrong time and place to deal with the issue, maybe in front of other staff or customers.
- The situation is one where tempers could flare in the heat of the moment, and people could get emotional and lose sight of the real issues.
- You need to talk to the person involved alone or with a third party.
- The conflict has wider implications that need to be considered before it is solved.

The important thing here is that the only sound reason for avoiding conflict now, when there clearly is an issue that needs exploring, is that this is a temporary measure. It still needs to be dealt with at a more suitable time.

Possum's law

■ ■ ■

Possums curl up on the ground and pretend to be dead when threatened by a predator. It works quite well. Eating rotten meat in a hot climate is a bad idea. So the crocodile wanders away in search of a different dinner. Problem solved. The possum lives to tell the tale – until next time!

The crocodiles of the business world don't go away quite so easily. Avoiding conflict by being passive reduces your level of anxiety in the short term. Agreeing to help someone out by taking on extra work may make you feel virtuous. Possums can't always play dead – one day the crocodile will get wise.

Passive behaviour ... for example

Let's look at a specific situation to illustrate some of the problems of passive behaviour.

Case study 2.2

TROUBLE AT THE TRACTOR FACTORY

Tom is an accountant in a tractor factory. Like most accountants he prepares financial reports and amends his forecasts every quarter. He's good at managing his workload but things always get a bit hectic as the next report deadline roles around.

Just before the third quarter report is due Tom's boss calls him up. He's just got back from a trip to Russia and is really excited about a possible new export deal. Could Tom have a look at the figures and come up with a financial recommendation by the end of the week?

The Russian deal sounds like a great opportunity – but what about the quarterly report?

So a manager like Tom is faced with an obvious problem – whether to comply entirely with the boss's wishes or to explain his position and see if a compromise can be reached.

Perhaps Tom would say 'It sounds exciting. I'm right in the middle of filing the quarterly figures, so things are really busy this week. But I could look at it on Monday?' If his boss is a reasonable man, he'll probably think that is a sensible compromise.

Imagine, however, that Tom's approach to the situation is passive. Read on:

Case study 2.2 Cont'd.

Tom pops up to his boss's office and finds him already in conversation with Ed, the new sales manager. 'Sorry – am I interrupting?'

'The Russian tractor market is wide open to European expansion. I know they've got roaring inflation but with a bit of careful sales talk, I'm sure we'll reach the profit margin we need', says Ed. Tom has his doubts. They'd need to talk to the Trade Delegation to estimate the real costs – but his boss must have thought of that. They both look at Tom hopefully. 'Well, maybe we should talk to a few people first – but I'm sure you're right.' He looks at his feet to avoid saying more.

'Here are the figures. We're meeting the bankers next week but I'd like your thoughts by tomorrow if that's OK?' Tom thought about the quarterly report – he'd have to work through the night if his boss thought it was so important. Better ring his wife and cancel going to the school play.

Ed got up to leave, 'Nice chap, Tom, but he doesn't say very much!'

Rather a different approach with very different consequences. Much of Tom's behaviour is typically passive, ignoring his own rights and submitting to the needs of another. The manager taking this course disregards whether or not his course of action is appropriate – it is simply the course of least conflict. Tom's behaviour is an extreme version of passive behaviour but it indicates many of the typical patterns which emerge in a passive approach to difficult situations. For example:

- *Body language* – Tom stares at his feet to avoid expressing his feelings. Other typical behaviour might include appearing to be engrossed in other people's views to avoid being questioned yourself; fidgeting nervously; hiding behind your hair; searching thoughtfully through paperwork, etc.
- *Not standing up for one's own rights* – Tom assumes his boss needs the report urgently, making no attempt to state his own position. Managers need to prioritise in the light of real facts, not

emotions, so postponing, advancing or delegating work is a sound business decision reflecting the current state of resources.

- *Thinking others' needs and rights are more important than one's own.* Tom assumes he doesn't have any rights and shows this by assuming he has to work through the night; managers faced with this form of subjugation will find it hard to know what they are dealing with.
- *Apologising* – the passive individual will tend to apologise constantly. This makes it hard for his or her manager; in Tom's case the apology was unnecessary in the first place.
- *Not contributing his ideas* – passive people tend to think their own ideas are worthless anyway!
- *Not being honest about the situation* – sad but true of the mess a passive response to a situation can get people into.
- *Feeling anxious about there being too much work to do* – probably familiar to most people.

Aggressive behaviour

■ ■ ■

Assertiveness is often confused with aggression. People think that assertiveness means getting what you want, rather than reaching the best possible conclusion for all concerned.

Aggressive office colleagues are much like the school playground bully. They trample on the smaller kids and don't listen to anyone else's feelings. They order you around and make you run errands for them or do their homework. They act tough and threaten to knock you down if you don't do what they want. The aggresive person is often a quite obvious problem and can take up a lot of time and energy to manage.

It's the same when we grow up and go to work. Aggressive managers are authoritarian and rarely listen to reasoned argument. They bully staff into taking on ludicrous workloads or targets which cannot possibly be delivered. Then they get angry, rant and rave when these targets are not met.

Anger can provoke all sorts of different reactions – including anger itself. Common reactions include feeling:

- intimidated,
- frightened,
- being controlled,
- losing control and starting to play the game by their rules,
- embarrassed,
- inadequate.

When the situation has calmed down other feelings begin to take over, such as anger and frustration that you gave in, or didn't think to handle the problem in a different way. How often have we relived an argument, kicked ourselves and asked, 'Why didn't I say that?'.

The effects of aggressive behaviour on individuals

■ ■ ■

Like passivity, being aggressive is also a short-term approach to conflict. It may 'solve' the immediate problem by achieving the desired result and give an initial feeling of elation and power.

Long term, most aggressive individuals will experience as many doubts as the passive person. It is likely they will start to feel guilty about their behaviour. They may expect the colleagues they have vanquished to get their own back and so become defensive and constantly on the alert. Indeed, that may not be an unrealistic expectation. In the long run aggression tends to provoke further aggression – as the saying goes, 'Don't get mad, get even'.

Most people know if they tell their manager to get knotted, they may provoke a major argument, or even get to collect their P45. They don't need to worry when dealing with subordinates or those with no direct control over their work. Or do they? It is easy to lose respect for someone who constantly loses his or her temper. That can have damaging consequences for such a person's reputation within the company, regardless of how fair that judgement is. Take the following example:

Case study 2.3

THE GORGON

A senior manager in a international dealing house had quite a reputation. She was greatly respected as the first woman on the firm's board of directors – but also renowned for her fearsome temper. New recruits to her department rarely lasted longer than a few months. Colleagues even took to running a book on how long they would last.

In reality, whilst she was prone to fly off the handle, she was a good boss. She delegated tasks and took the time to tell her trainees how they were doing and what they could do better. She gave juniors full credit for jobs they had done well and made sure that the rest of the management and her clients knew about it. Sadly, what people remembered was her ferocious temper and her nickname, 'The Gorgon'.

The effects of aggressive behaviour on the organisation

■ ■ ■

For organisations the effects of aggressive behaviour can be manifest. It can cause in-fighting between people and departments and be a needless diversion for the manager.

The following is, again, based on a story told to us on a training course.

> *'We had one MD and two directors in our organisation. One of the directors was a horror. She would humiliate people in front of their colleagues and friends. She would pile work on people's desks right at the end of the day and tell people to finish it before they went home. I had this once on my wedding anniversary and I was meant to be going to the theatre. Worse still, you wouldn't see her for days as she'd be on the computer in her office and then she's suddenly be on the prowl.*

'One senior manager was once reduced to tears by a rollicking he took from her. It really destroyed morale. Loads of people left. And this was because the big boss refused to manage the problem. We would go into his room and he would listen patiently. He'd promise to talk to the person in question, but nothing happened. We lost all respect for him. Eventually I moved on, I couldn't stand it any more. But her aggression must have cost the organisation tens of thousands of pounds in terms of having to recruit new people and simply not getting the best out of people.'

David Crew of Midland Bank's equal opportunities department believes that aggression in the workplace is a straightforward business issue. It costs the bank time and money.

'There are moral and ethical dimensions to it, but (when looking at allegations of harassment) we go beyond that to look at what harassment, bullying, victimisation and other forms of non-physical violence actually cost the business. ... Aggression in the workplace leads to sickness, absenteeism, low morale and more errors – the very things that managers spend their lives trying to prevent.'

The line between strong managerial style and bullying can be quite fine. The key is whether what is said is firm and constructive or destructive. In extreme cases aggression can become harassment based on power and its abuse. The power of the aggressor could be status, physical strength, personality, age, numbers, or knowledge about the victim. As Crew points out, 'Any large organisation will have aggression in all its forms, because it's got people in it. By the law of averages, some of those people will display aggression. Any organisation that doesn't think it's got a problem is kidding itself'.

So how do aggressive people see the world? Well, they

- ignore other people's feelings or beliefs,
- stand up for their own rights but violate the rights of other people,
- see situations as being about winning or losing.

And this is important because with aggressive behaviour you often get a win–lose situation. The aggressive person may feel that he or she has won, but everyone else and the organisation loses.

Case study 2.4

AGGRESSIVE BEHAVIOUR ... FOR EXAMPLE

Allegedly, one of the most legendary (or perhaps infamous) aggressive managers of recent years was Robert Maxwell. Many of his past employees have confessed to being intimidated by him, often living in actual fear of his next pronouncement or action.

One of the Maxwell Group's former senior executives described Maxwell's style of management as a three-pronged approach – isolation, humiliation and decapitation! Not a style other managers should seek to emulate!

A couple of alleged incidents typify Maxwell's aggressive nature. He once complained he couldn't afford to give his secretary time off to get married. If she had to have the day off she must take the mobile phone with her so he could get in touch. On the great day Maxwell phoned his secretary at exactly the time she was due to walk down the aisle. There was no reply. She had switched the phone off and for her disloyalty was sacked.

On another occasion, Maxwell allegedly walked into the office of the Mirror Group's company secretary, a highly respected official of 20 years' standing, to find him ripping up a small piece of paper. 'Stop', yelled Maxwell, 'You're destroying company property'. In fact it was an old change of address card but Maxwell would not be placated and stormed out.

Hopefully, such extremism is an exception. He was the kind of grandaddy of aggressive managers. However, as we've seen, aggression can rear its ugly head at any time at work.

Let's examine the following example and see what happened.

Case study 2.5

AGGRESSIVE BEHAVIOUR ... ANOTHER EXAMPLE

Kate was an editor in a busy publishing house. She enjoyed her work but found it hard to work for her manager Donna, who constantly lost her temper.

▶

> One day Donna called Kate into her office. An important client was visiting tomorrow and she simply didn't have time to prepare the presentation for them. Kate could do it, couldn't she? Kate explained she had an editing deadline to meet that day and asked if the client would be given the standard company presentation. If so, her secretary knew what was needed and could be relied on to do a good job.
>
> Donna got up and started to shout and thump the table. 'I don't want a wet-behind-the-ears secretary to do it – I want you. I have deadlines to meet as well you know. And if I want your advice I'll ask for it – you're not paid to solve personnel problems.'
>
> Somewhat taken aback, Kate dared to mention that a delay in her report would cause severe problems in the Paris office. They were meeting the author that afternoon.
>
> 'I don't care, just do it', said Donna and stormed off to lunch with her friend.

The implications of this approach are considerable – frustrated and demoralised staff, disrupted schedules throughout the company and loss of trust and respect. Let's look these typical consequences of aggressive behaviour in more detail:

- *Ignoring/dismissing the needs, opinions, feelings or beliefs of others* – yours are far more important. Managers adopting this approach tend to lose the respect of their staff and may often miss out on vital information or ideas which could benefit their business.
- *Expressing your own needs, wants, opinions (which may be honest or dishonest) in inappropriate ways* – Donna maintained she was too busy to prepare the presentation, but not so busy she couldn't go out to a social lunch. This was, in effect, a form of manipulation, packaging the facts in a distorted way to serve your own ends. We'll look at this in more detail in the next section.
- *You have rights, other people don't* – a dangerous premise likely to result in never ending disputes. This attitude can be especially

damaging when managing people, for example when you need to persuade someone to take on more responsibility.

- *You have something to contribute* – nobody else does. Despite the validity of Kate's suggestion it is rejected out of hand. Again, this myopic approach leads to missed opportunities.
- *Body language and vocal approach* – Donna's approach is to shout and act dramatically; other ways include towering over people, bearing down on them or restricting the space they occupy, or perhaps excessive sarcasm.
- *Violating the rights of others* – whether these are personal, social or set out in a person's terms of employment, everyone is entitled to and has rights. We'll look at this issue in more detail in Chapter 3.

Violence in the workplace

The most extreme expression of aggressive behaviour is violence. Sadly, it is not as rare as we might care to think.

A survey carried out by the Institute of Personnel and Development in 1995 revealed that 11 per cent of workers had observed workplace violence during the last year. Over half of these had personally been involved in the incident. Furthermore, in 23 per cent of the reported incidents it was the manager who was violent.

When it comes to extreme aggression in the form of violence, employers may be legally liable. So managers who experience this difficulty within their team should refer the problem to their human resources department.

Manipulative behaviour

■ ■ ■

Aggression needn't always be that obvious. Sometimes the victim only realises that he or she has been the focus of aggression after having walked away from the situation. This is the aggressor as manipulator. Remember, assertiveness is about respecting the rights of others, as well as establishing your own rights, so plotting to get your own way is just as negative as outright aggression.

The manipulator plots to get their own way whatever the cost, usually at the expense of others. Facts are rarely black and white – they come in various different shades of grey depending on the picture the individual wants to paint. It is hard to pin the manipulator down and get to the heart of the matter. The aggressor will state plainly how they want things to be, but the manipulator has a hidden agenda. You may only discover what they want once you've agreed to it!

The manipulator plays the power game at work completely to their own advantage. They may well manoeuvre and talk behind your back. They may spread rumours. They will do anything to get on at anyone's expense.

There is another side to manipulative behaviour. Some people manipulate other's feelings without even knowing it. They play on their supposed vulnerability in order to get people to do what they want.

Quite common with manipulative behaviour is emotional blackmail.

Case study 2.6

THE SULKY CHILD

Toddlers are brilliant at getting their own way. Confronted by a plate of spinach (and with a nice chocolate pudding in the fridge), they hang their heads and look at you tearfully as if to say, 'How could you be so cruel?'. Generations of parents have tried to stick to their guns – but once in a while most of us give in. Suddenly the child is all smiles. They know they have a great future career as a con artist!

The office sulky child is the same. Burdened down by piles of work, they lead a terrible life. Offer a helping hand – and a full in-tray full is dumped on your desk. Oddly, they always get away with it.

This behaviour need not be motivated by malice. Often it is simply instinctive, a way of quickly fixing a problem they don't really want to handle.

Ultimately this form of manipulation leads to built-up resentment amongst other team members. Manipulation may take the form of dumping work, avoiding responsibility, getting better perks or simply stirring up gossip. It can also be hard to trust the sulky child, as their tasks are re-delegated without responsible guidance or facts are tailored to suit their own ends.

Aiming for win-win using assertive behaviour

■ ■ ■

And finally we look at some basics about assertive behaviour and confirm what we started the chapter with – what the 'A word' actually means.

Having looked at the alternatives, we hope you have a clear view now of what assertiveness is, because rarely has a word been so misunderstood. People think it actually means aggression – getting what you want. Others think assertiveness is for wimps. As you know, neither is true.

So why has assertiveness been so often misunderstood? Maybe because it has been overused in the past few years, and has become devalued – there are lots of courses and books around, and they are not all excellent. Maybe because it developed much of its status in specific issues, like equal opportunities for women, and is still seen by many men as being about that. Again, this is not the case – it's for everyone.

Assertiveness is about answers to some difficult and fundamental questions about the way individuals behave towards each other.

There are as many definitions of assertiveness as there are books on the subject, but all have some key points in common. Some of these are that assertiveness:

- is based on an acceptance of other people's rights and responsibilities,

- is based just as much on an acceptance of the fact that you have as many rights and responsibilities as they do,
- means biting the bullet and being honest with other people, and with yourself,
- requires you to say clearly and without anger what you believe, want or think. So it is about speaking your mind openly and objectively,
- requires you to know your own mind and politely and clearly communicate what you want,
- is not about hurting other people or getting the better of them – not about winners and losers but all about everyone winning,
- involves negotiation and compromise to reach solutions that are acceptable all round. It does not involve emotional blackmail.

Looking at the number of times this list contains words like 'knowing', believe' 'rights' and 'responsibilities' shows clearly that assertiveness is a philosophy or a set of values and beliefs, rather than just a series of techniques and quick fixes.

But if you act assertively you will be able to:

- Say 'No';
- Stand up for your beliefs and interests while taking account of other people and respecting what they think, feel, believe and want.

The interesting thing is that in many ways assertiveness does not seem to come 'naturally' to most of us. It something we have to work on. So we have to work at managing our feelings about conflict, learn how to say 'No' and stand up for our rights.

And why do we say that assertiveness is win–win? Well, because it is just that. With assertiveness you win because you have had your say, respected yourself, listened to others, negotiated and compromised. But everyone else wins too. The people you are assertive with, and your organisation also get a win out of it too.

The difference between assertiveness and aggression

People often do get confused between aggression and assertiveness. However, the differences are really quite obvious.

The following example gives a flavour of how assertiveness can work. In the rest of this book we look at how to really develop this skill for yourself.

Winning through with assertiveness

■ ■ ■

The crucial thing is that handling difficult situations assertively should help the manager to reach a win–win situation. The assertive approach will enable you to sit down calmly with your boss and examine all the pros and cons of an awkward situation. You can decide what you both really need to achieve and come up with a solution which keeps everyone happy. The great thing is that it's surprising how often assertiveness can bring out new ideas. Assertive behaviour can stop a problem being a problem by turning it into an opportunity.

Case study 2.7

ASSERTIVENESS ... FOR EXAMPLE

Tessa was a very popular secretary, always smiling and keeping the office happy. She worked hard and was always willing to help out – but little things began to go wrong. She made careless mistakes, was abrupt with clients on the phone and forgot to book certain appointments when asked.

One day, quite out of the blue, Tessa snapped. She announced to the whole department that she'd had enough, was going to get another job and stalked out of the office.

Managers facing this situation could choose to resolve it in various different ways:

- *passively* – by ignoring the outburst, presuming Tessa was just having a bad day,
- *aggressively* – by calling her into their office and demanding an explanation,

or

- *manipulatively* – by deciding to encourage her to leave. You never really liked her anyway and that new typist would be much easier to work with.

None of these approaches would necessarily be wrong. But would they achieve an outcome that gave everyone the best results? If Tessa's boss followed any of the routes above, the organisation loses a valuable employee, Tessa loses a job, the manager loses someone who knows what to do and why … and the costs of finding and training a replacement could be extremely high. So surely the only sensible approach is to talk it through and see if there is something that can save the day – putting pride and anger to one side.

Case study 2.7 Cont'd.

Tessa's manager was as perplexed as everyone else by the outburst. No one thought Tessa was worried about anything. So he decided to talk to her at the first suitable opportunity.

The next day, to celebrate a successful project, he took the team out for a pub lunch. He congratulated them for doing a great job and made a particular point of thanking the two team secretaries for coping so well.

Later that day he called Tessa into his office for a chat. He expressed his concern over recent events and gradually got Tessa to tell him what was bothering her.

It turned out she felt trapped in her job. She was bored. What she really wanted to do was develop the team's sales presentations. They could do so much more with the computer system and in the long run it would save everyone time. She was sure she could still handle her current work at the same time.

The manager asked Tessa to put her ideas on paper and if her plans made sense for the section, perhaps a test period would work.

Someone had to make the first move and break the deadlock. The manager in this case acted assertively and recognised there was more to lose by doing nothing. Tackling the situation in this way meant the manager could:

- *stand up for his own rights and needs but take others into account* – the work still needs doing, but acknowledging the other person's viewpoint may reveal factors you cannot predict, changing the situation entirely;
- *express his needs, opinions and feelings in direct, honest and appropriate ways* – by stating honestly that Tessa was a valued team member, but her work was not up to scratch at the moment;
- *be reasoned and calm about discussing things* – rational discussion is rarely possible when people are angry. It's much better to defuse the situation, or leave it until later. More gets achieved when all parties are calm;
- *contributing your views and ideas and listening/encouraging those of others* – because Tessa felt able to be honest about her ideas and opportunity opened up to develop Tessa and to help the department. It's always worth listening, even if you reject the idea after discussing it.

In the event, Tessa's problem can be seen as a build-up of frustration over time and not just a one-off situation. So although the manager tackled this situation well, what a difference there would have been if the normal approach in the office had been one where everyone felt able to say what they felt, without being constrained by passive or aggressive feelings. Then Tessa could have calmly and sensibly discussed the situation with her boss and they could have worked towards a successful solution much earlier.

However, even at the eleventh hour when faced by a potentially aggressive, destructive scenario the manager's assertive approach enabled him to re-motivate Tessa, avoid further disruption (especially in having to recruit another secretary) and benefit his team. Ignoring the situation or letting Tessa walk out of the door would only have created more problems in the long run.

Some heretical thoughts

■ ■ ■

Some books on assertiveness will tell you it is the answer to everything in the universe. Indeed, we believe that assertiveness is a really positive and worthwhile approach and can be of real help, not just at work, but in the rest of life too. We also believe that being assertive helps in an agenda for personal growth and development.

It sounds odd to say, but growing is hard. Not growing up in terms of how old we are, because no one has much say in that. What we are talking about is really growing – this means being more complete people, more able to deal with what life throws at us.

But that said, don't fall into the trap of believing that assertiveness is a universal cure. Simply, it is guff to suggest that assertiveness will do for every situation, although it is generally the best approach and clearly a better alternative to caving in or blowing up. There are times when being passive, aggressive or manipulative fits the bill and is an appropriate response. It is impossible to specify when these situations may arise – all we're saying is that you do not have to change your personality and turn into some strange being you don't recognise. Just be assertive whenever it's appropriate – which is a good deal of the time.

But think about it. Sometimes assertiveness may not be right.

Another Bob Maxwell story, inspired by the illuminating, funny and frankly scary book called *Maxwell Stories*, by Sam Jaffa, from which our earlier examples were drawn, shows the impotence of assertiveness in some situations. If you come across a totally autocratic boss, the answer may be just to quit. Sometimes when confronted with real might, submission is what is required. Take the story of the rhino.

Case study 2.8

RHINO ON THE RUN

Back in the 1980s Bob Maxwell visited Africa on one of his overseas missions. He decided he wanted to have his photo taken in the bush and so headed out in a jeep with a gaggle of photographers. After a while he spotted in the distance a herd of rhinos. He left the jeep with the warnings of a park warden ringing in his ears about how dangerous rhinos could be.

After a moment or two, one of the rhinos spotted Maxwell and made his way over. Shortly, the journalists were cowering in the jeep as the rhino started to get very near. Eventually the rhino and Maxwell (who, of course, bore more than a passing resemblance to the rhino itself) were nose to horn. The clamour from the jeep was deafening, although one brave person did get the snap. Eventually, taking a look into the eye of Maxwell, our friend the rhino decided he didn't fancy taking him on and ran off.

If you are in a situation when you are facing a metaphorical rhino (or a real one for that matter), running off may be the answer.

On the flip side of the coin, manipulation is sometimes useful and indeed the only response possible. For instance, sometimes when introducing a major change managers need to indulge in a little manipulation in order to make it work.

And finally ... handling the aftermath of conflict

■ ■ ■

Finally in this chapter, it is important to think through carefully how to handle the aftermath of conflict. There are lots of books on assertiveness that tell you how to avoid conflict, but what do you do if and when it breaks out?

The following is how one person described the messy business of conflict aftermath.

> *'We had a really tough time at work. We had loads of evening meetings and friction between management and staff. It was terrible.*

'But through it all me and my boss were a real team. We supported each other and really had a kind of spirit of the Blitz. Because we are both women and it's a man's world, it did feel like a team.

'One day when the real trouble at work died down we were doing a leaflet drop and over nothing at all we started to argue. It was very civilised, but it was an argument none the less. When I got home I felt really upset by what had happened.'

What would you do in this situation? It's painful and upsetting, but then again conflict normally is. Let's wind forward and see how the manager resolved things.

'I sat at home and thought, dammit no, I refuse to fall out over something like this. So I picked up the phone and rang my boss at home. I told her that I didn't enjoy the argument and that it felt horrible. She immediately said how glad she was I had rung and that she felt horrible too.

'We then spoke about the argument and agreed that either of us may have been right and that we should put it behind us. I felt very good about this and I felt vindicated in my belief that as a grown-up it is OK to say, it hurts but let's move on.'

This is a classic resolution and is based on:

- acknowledging that conflict is painful,
- acknowledging we have a right to feel and express hurt,
- understanding that both sides can be right in an argument,
- making clear that the argument has not downgraded one's respect for the other person,
- a commitment to be open and honest and then to move on.

It's time for the second window on assertiveness.

Window 2

HANDLING AGGRESSION – WHY ASSERTIVENESS WORKS

'For me learning how to be assertive, effectively, was a life-saving skill. Working in an auction house you need to be able to build good relationships with customers, quickly. The first point of contact with a customer is often when they bring an item in to be valued or buy something at auction. You only have a few minutes to build a good rapport and make sure that yours is the auction house they bring their business to next time.

'Auction days can be fraught – chaotic, queues of impatient clients and hundreds of lots to clear and pack. You must be polite but you've got to keep people under control – that means being really assertive.

'When I worked at Christie's one of my most "difficult" clients was a German toy and doll collector from Germany. A regular buyer at auction, he always wanted to pack the lots into his car immediately after the sale and drive straight back to Germany. We usually had at least 50 other clients to deal with, so we would have to ask him to wait. He'd get really annoyed, raise his voice, thump the table – the worst problem was he only spoke German and although the gist of it was obvious none of us really understood him!

'I realise now that the tactics I employed were in fact classic assertiveness techniques. Tone and presentation was vital – I could say, "I'm sorry Sir. You'll have to wait five minutes but we will help you then", but I couldn't guarantee he actually understood what I was saying! I'd speak calmly and softly, look him straight in the eyes and smile a lot. It was always a bit of a battle but in the long run we'd get through – and he would reappear at the next auction.

'Years later, I came across this gentlemen again at another auction house. This time I spoke German. It was quite a revelation – it turned out he could speak English after all. He never admitted it because he felt he got his own way more often if he just yelled in German – the English never argued back, they were passive and just gave in! Undoubtedly true, but he annoyed a lot of people too. Sad really, he was really quite a pleasant chap.'

3

Where are you now?

Doing the diagnostic

We've talked about natural styles and examined the different types – passive, aggressive, manipulative and assertive – in greater detail. We've also looked at some of the sticking points people face day-to-day: the kind of things that trip them up and they find difficult to handle.

The next step is to think clearly about yourself. You need to be clear:

- how you behave at the moment in certain situations,
- what you would like to improve,
- how you are going to do it.

Although there are distinctive styles, the likelihood is that your own approach is a combination of styles. A bit of a curate's egg – good in parts. Perhaps you find it easy to calm people down but hard to tell someone bad news? Maybe asking for advice is fine but saying 'No' is impossible? The good thing about this curate's egg is that, by learning to be more assertive, you can make the bad parts better.

The questionnaires and case studies in this chapter are designed to help you pinpoint where in your working life you may want to be more assertive. This chapter is essentially a diagnostic tool. We'll look at some of the typical problems facing today's front-line manager and help you to identify issues you would like to handle more effectively.

Each scenario could be approached in many different ways – you may think of alternative solutions to those in the questionnaire. The important thing is to discover how you, as a manager, feel most comfortable in dealing with this particular problem and, of course, where you want to go to next.

Try to be honest with yourself. There is a great deal of difference between knowing what you should do to get the best out of a situation and actually putting it into practice. It's all too easy to shy away from the assertive approach because you fear the implications. Disagree with the boss and will you be penalised? Tell someone their work is below par and will they hate you or cause difficulties in the department?

So it's important for managers to identify the situations which they feel less confident about handling so they can develop a more positive approach. Think of this chapter as a road map. It will help you to decide where you want to get to and how you intend to get there.

By the end of this chapter you should have pinpointed the areas on which you want to concentrate. Through the rest of the book we will move on to look at ways in which you can strengthen your approach in these areas.

1. You and your manager

Conflict with your manager can be very damaging. However, it is one of the main areas in which conflict can and does take place at work. People are likely to be less assertive in relationships where they are the junior partner (you and your manager). After all, at the end of the day it is your manager who tends to wield rather a lot of power. If you have an assertive approach to working with your manager, you are more likely to be assertive elsewhere, for example, when sorting out problems with your colleagues or people that you manage.

But dealing with your manager is about far more than dealing with conflict. In normal circumstances there isn't conflict. But the key is to learn how to manage your manager and get the very best from the relationship – in peacetime and during war!

It is important to point out that the relationship between you and your manager is probably the single most important relationship you have at work. You probably don't need to be told this because just about everyone has had the unfortunate experience of not really hitting it off with the manager.

This is one pretty typical horror story.

> *'When I started working for my manager it really seemed good. However, over time niggles started to come into play. He always seemed to be displeased with what I did.*
>
> *'Eventually my manager's manager called me into an office and said that it wasn't working because there was a personality clash between me and my boss. I was really upset and said that I didn't actually clash with him, he was doing all the clashing with me.'*

Let's examine your relationship with your own manager. How good is it? What could do with improving? You could start by doing the following:

- Make a list of some of the issues which can, do or might lead to conflict between you and your line manager. Alongside each one make any notes you can about what you do to overcome or avoid them.

- Finally, look back at your list and mark those issues which you feel you would like to handle better in the future.

The possible list is wide – poor communication; either side taking inappropriate decisions; feeling hurt when ideas are rejected; letting small disagreements or upsets get out of hand before you act to limit the damage. The exercise is important because it should alert you to whether this is a particular area you need to work on.

The answers you gave and how you feel about handling these issues will be personal to you.

However, they should have started you thinking about the kinds of conflicts you may need to manage and some of the challenges you face. In the rest of this chapter we will look at some of the specific issues you may have noted.

As you read through the chapter make a note of those issues you want to handle better in the future.

2. Saying 'No' (or 'Yes' when you want to)

■ ■ ■

Why is it so hard to say 'No'? It can be a real stumbling block. Confronted by an unwanted invitation, a request you're too busy to deal with, an ill-considered proposal, you're unable to say 'No'. You make excuses, tell white lies, ignore telephone messages, anything to avoid just saying 'No'.

Afraid of what the person asking you might do, think or feel (and, most importantly, about think about you) you do the opposite of what you intend and say 'Yes'! It gets you out of the immediate situation. The problems arise when, later, you succumb to feelings guilt or pettiness. Ultimately you've dodged the problem, not dealt with it and that means it's likely to be even worse the next time it arises.

Imagine that the boss asks you to jump three feet into the air from a standing start. You can manage two feet, or can make three feet with a run up. But you simply are physically unable to meet the demand. What do you do? Many people will say, 'I'll do my best'. The trouble is, you know before you even try that your best isn't good enough, so the only possible outcome is failure.

If this scenario sounds all too familiar, assertiveness could help you to confront the problem. You need to ask yourself whether you are someone who has real trouble saying 'No'.

Look at the following examples and think how you would react:

Questionnaire 3.1

WHAT DOES IT TAKE FOR YOU TO SAY 'NO'?

Q1 Your boss asks you deputise for him at a departmental meeting. You've arranged to see an important client and you don't want to cancel. Do you:

- **(a)** Say 'No'? Explain it's the only day the client can see you this month – and their order is due for renewal? ❒
- **(b)** Say you'll go and then worry about it, and try to fix a different date with the client? ❒
- **(c)** Snap back that it's really inconvenient. Someone else will have to go? ❒

Q2 A colleague asks if they can have your sales figures by lunchtime instead of at the end of the day. Do you:

- **(a)** Say 'No' – they'll be ready by 5 p.m. but you've got to do some other work first? ❒
- **(b)** Say 'Yes' and work through lunch? ❒
- **(c)** Say they must be joking and walk away? ❒

Q3 Your boss tells you to warn his secretary formally about her lax attitude to work. He's going out and hasn't got time. Do you :

- **(a)** Explain that you don't think it's appropriate – it is better coming from him tomorrow? ❒
- **(b)** Make feeble attempts to back out but fail. Then worry about how you're going to handle it? ❒
- **(c)** Agree to do it – nothing like watching people squirm! ❒

Q4 The junior accountant asks if you can finish off a spread sheet for her. Do you:

- **(a)** Say 'No' but suggest you go through her final draft together to sort out any problems? ❒

(b) Say 'Yes' – it'll take too long to explain it to her and you want her to feel warm towards you? ❒

(c) Get angry because she had the temerity to ask you? ❒

Q5 You've just told your boss you can't take on any more work. You're overloaded already. Do you feel:

(a) Happy – you both discussed the situation and found another way round the problem? ❒

(b) Worried – saying 'No' will be a black mark on your record? ❒

(c) Angry – they ought to know how hard you work? ❒

Organisations can make it very hard for managers to put their needs and those of their teams first. Deadlines, budget requirements, reporting structures and the needs of other departments all add to the convoluted picture. However, sometimes these excuses provide a convenient smoke screen. They enable us to ignore the real reason for failing to say no.

Deeper personal reasons include lack of self-esteem or a poor self-image. If you worry about telling your boss that a request is unreasonable (Questions 1, 3 or 5) is it because you don't think your opinion counts? Or because you have a bad relationship with your boss?

Guilt can produce different reactions. In Question 2 a passive person may have decided to work through lunch – they'd feel bad if they didn't help, or maybe they owed their colleague a favour. Alternatively guilt can emerge as an aggressive response. Does an angry response to a subordinate's request for help actually convey guilt – you feel your team leadership skills are lacking or you haven't trained a new recruit well enough?

It is also hard to say 'No' when you are afraid of what others will think of you. Often, it's difficult to separate personal feelings from business transactions. How many of us could say, honestly, that we've never agreed to do something we probably shouldn't because we liked the person who asked? It's a short step to worrying too much about other people's opinions. Let this reaction get out of control and you could end up doing exactly the opposite of what you think is right. The next section looks at some of the blockages this fear can cause.

Judging your general approach

There is also a general theme to these answers. If you chose mostly Answer A, you already tend towards an assertive approach. Most of these answers express your rights and needs as a manager, leaving the way open for the person asking you to discuss his or her rights and needs. Question 3 is the least flexible scenario.

If you are a reasonably assertive manager, congratulations! The detailed discussions of negotiation, constructive feedback and specific assertiveness techniques in later chapters may give you some ideas as to how to be even better.

Mainly B answers indicate that you tend to be passive. Sometimes this may be appropriate – perhaps the departmental meeting in Question 1 was crucial, so rearranging to see the client was the lesser of two evils. Remember, saying 'No' can be absolutely justifiable. Just because the boss says so, you don't go out and shoot yourself!

Managers who tend to express themselves forcefully will choose mostly C answers. Again, sometimes managers need to put their foot down. Perhaps the junior accountant in Question 4 is perfectly able to produce spread sheets but never takes responsibility for her work. An assertive approach (Answer A) might provide greater benefits. It could help the manager get to the root of the problem and prevent it happening again.

Managers who feel their personal style is a little too passive or aggressive and want an alternative approach will find Chapter 6 helpful. It looks at developing basic assertiveness, the very basic approach of saying what you feel without giving offence. One issue you will read about there is something that applies when you want to say 'No' – relating to the example of jumping three feet in the air. Saying that you can't do one thing ... but you can do another is still saying 'No', but it softens the blow tremendously. It's one of the key elements in assertiveness – saying what you believe honestly and constructively, to reach a satisfactory outcome.

So once again, how did you rate. Is learning to say 'No' a real one you need to work on?

3. Conquering the fear of being disliked

Management can get very personal. Often it's tempting to take the easy route out of a problem because people will like you for it. Taking on excessive workloads to please your boss (or your team) is typical.

So the next step is to see whether one of your stumbling blocks is the need to overcome the fear of being disliked. If you find it a stumbling block, take heart, you are not alone.

Case study 3.1

FRIENDSHIP OR MARTYRDOM – THAT IS THE QUESTION!

Carolyn worked with a consultant, organising a major concert with an international line-up of performers, for six months. They were some of the worst of her life!

'I was the only person from my company working on the event. So it was important that I had a good personal relationship with the consultant. She was a forceful character (and I was new to the company), so it was hard to disagree with her.

'The consultant believed that, to run a successful event, you needed to work 18 hours a day, seven days a week. In reality, you need to work hard, but you can get things done without being a martyr. I didn't like to challenge her early on in case we fell out. The problem was, when I did challenge her, she'd sulk or get angry. Sometimes we agreed a compromise – then she would phone me at home and use an entire answerphone tape explaining why I had to do things her way!

'I realise now that avoiding confrontation early in the event was a mistake. I don't know if tackling the problem would have changed her attitude. But it would certainly have made my job easier – and saved time dealing with the same old argument over and over again.'

It happens to managers too

Sometimes it comes as a shock to newly promoted managers that, suddenly, they're no longer one of the gang, privy to the office gossip and chit-chat. Like it or not, the us and them syndrome still exists in many organisations.

In the long run doing anything and everything to stay in favour will cause managers greater problems, not to mention a loss of respect. On the other hand, it does no harm to take other people's opinions into account – you may learn something.

Self-test 3.1

HOW WOULD YOU REACT?

How would you react to these two situations and why?

1 Imagine your department is discussing plans for a new office layout. Everyone seems to agree that privacy is important. They want their own space to be partitioned off. A couple of people haven't said anything.

Personally, you believe an open-plan office would improve communications. You're in charge but would you be the one dissenting voice?

2 The marketing director has had a brain wave. He's decided that all company cars should be bright pink! Do you rush out and paint your own car pink? Maybe you should borrow a paint chart and ask what other colours he thinks might look good (preferably dark blue!) Or perhaps just tell him straight that everyone thinks it's a ludicrous idea?

He's a bit of a tricky character. No one seems to want to confront him. What do you do?

Fear of what others think stops some people from stepping forward and expressing a different point of view. Say nothing and you avoid confrontation, but you will end up hating yourself … and your pink car. Alternatively, managers who leap in and forcefully express their viewpoint may suppress good ideas from their team. Worse still, they may be completely oblivious of strong feelings which will affect the performance of their department.

Management as a role

One approach that helps avoid the fear of personal dislike is consciously to remove as much personal baggage from the scene as possible. It's not easy but, with practice and frequent reminders, it can make a real difference.

It boils down to the fact that we all play many roles during our lives – even during a single day. One minute we're a parent to our children, the next we're a child to our parents. Or one minute we're a customer, then we're selling something. In one situation we're teaching others, in the next situation we're learners ourselves. With our boss we're a junior, with our team we're the boss.

Without even realising it, we shift from role to role without a great deal of fuss or trouble. Except, that is, when our emotions surface and we have an overwhelming desire to be liked. Then we blur the edges and mix up the roles.

Case study 3.2

ERIC AND ERICA

Eric started a job as a sales representative. He was popular, lively and everyone thought he'd do really well. But after a few weeks the results showed he was just not getting the orders.

Erica, the boss, went with him for a few calls and watched what happened. When they sat in the café afterwards, discussing why

Eric hadn't pulled off any sales, they came to the heart of the matter. He simply had not asked for any orders. Sure, he'd been affable and friendly, but his aim seemed to be to get the chance to come back – it was as if he felt that if he didn't ask for an order nobody could reject him.

This is a remarkably common problem with sales staff. It is a situation where the customer saying 'No' to an order is taken as a personal statement. If you don't ask, at least they can't reject you – and nobody wants to be rejected.

But look at it from the other side. How do you expect a sales assistant in a shop to act? As if the most important issue was whether you liked them, or in the role of a professional, helping you make a sensible buying decision? We have a mental checklist of what we expect sales assistants to do and we get confused if they act out of that role. Basically, we need them to be the sort of sales assistant we expect to meet.

It's the same with doctors and lawyers. They may have to tell us bad news, but because it's their job we don't blame them personally. In fact, if they hold back bad news because they think we will be upset, we blame them for being unprofessional. It's the role they play and the role we expect.

Case study 3.2 Cont'd.

On the following Monday Eric started with a new drive, following some useful advice and a bit of coaching from Erica. He did what he knew sales representatives did, looking the part, explaining benefits of products and asking for orders. It was very shaky at first, but after the first call, when the buyer didn't place an order but seemed quite happy to arrange for Eric to call back next month, the truth started to dawn.

The buyer saw Eric as a professional – a nice guy as well – but primarily a professional. He expected Eric to try and make a sale

▶

and wanted to be helped to buy if the products would benefit him and his firm. The buyer actually seemed more friendly and comfortable with Eric's sharper and focused selling approach than he had with his previous attempts to avoid asking for any firm decisions. After all, making firm decisions was the business the buyer was in.

Eric still got an invitation to their Christmas party, so they must have liked him as well.

Managers are no different. Try this simple check.

Self-test 3.2

THE WORST AND THE BEST

Stop and think for a minute of the worst and least effective manager you have ever worked for. Try and pinpoint what made them that bad, in your eyes. Then try it for the best manager you have ever met.

From whichever standpoint you look at it, the chances are that the only connection between good management and whether they tried to please everyone was a negative feeling – that any manager who tries to appease everyone ends up pleasing nobody, and can't make decisions. Perhaps one of the most damning comments you hear about ineffective managers is that they're useless ... 'but a really nice person'. That's not what they're there for and it's not nearly enough.

If we did a survey on what people think are the characteristics of a good manager, the words that would come out are guaranteed to include: firm, fair, respect, communication, support, honest and consistent. 'Nice' just doesn't come into it.

Case study 3.3

YOU CAN PLEASE SOME OF THE PEOPLE ALL OF THE TIME ...

A manager in a Social Services department had 20 staff, working as a team. One was a disaster – always late, letting clients down and not doing the right paperwork.

For a whole year the manager tried everything, the main approach being to lower the standards expected of this individual so they could get it right. The manager saw it as his own personal problem, to motivate and get results from the employee. He feared upsetting the employee's colleagues and being universally unpopular if he addressed the issues frontally and got into conflict.

Eventually, enough was enough. The manager realised he couldn't solve the employee's problem and told one of the team almost apologetically that he was going to have to do something about it. The reaction he got shocked him. 'About time! We're all fed up with covering for him, and it's about time management managed.'

By trying to appease someone and avoiding acting as a manager, the manager had lost the respect of the rest of the team. And the individual would never have respected him, no matter how much he gave in. By taking the correct and appropriate action, the manager did what the rest of the team expected their manager to do, whoever it was. In the event, the troublesome employee resigned.

Acting in role can be hard – changing roles can be especially difficult for someone who was one of the gang on Friday and a manager on Monday, because everyone suddenly expects him to know all the answers, start acting as a manager and turn into a different person over the weekend. But inside it's the same human being, with the same insecurities.

You have to be true to yourself and your own convictions – attempt to run with the hare and hunt with the hounds and you end up with no friends. Remember the saying attributed to Abraham Lincoln:

'You can please some of the people all of the time, or all of the people some of the time ... but you can't please all of the people all of the time.'

If you could, we wouldn't need managers because there would be no decisions to take, no hard choices to make.

Effective management is all about looking at the options and deciding which route is best. That means never being afraid to express your opinion to senior management or people who report to you. They expect you to do that – it's what managers do. Just do it diplomatically. If you find yourself hesitating in similar situations, an assertive approach could help you overcome this barrier.

A recent description of the boss of a large national organisation went – 'The boss is a bit like Millwall; no one likes him but he doesn't care!'. That's hard to believe, because very few people like to be unpopular, but for someone in the firing line it's crucial to let the role take the strain.

So, once more, how do you rate? Are you one of these types or not?

4. Stating your point of view

■ ■ ■

There are always two sides to every story. Unfortunately, getting your point of view across can be extremely difficult. Sometimes people just don't seem to listen and at other times it seems as if you end up talking at cross-purposes because one of you hasn't got the picture clear.

There are two key issues:

- making sure effective communication is taking place,
- feeling confident enough to say what you believe when it is at odds with other people's views.

Let's look at these two issues in a bit more depth.

Communication

When someone wants to pursue a course of action that you genuinely believe to be wrong, you want to put your point across and to do this you must establish clear communication or you have no chance of success. But we all have to communicate all day every day, so we must all be naturally gifted communicators, surely? Unfortunately not.

Communication is a two-way process.

Definition

COMMUNICATION

Communication has been described as: transferring information from one individual or group to another, so that it can be understood and acted on.

Think about this – especially the bit about 'being acted on'. Telling someone something does not necessarily mean they have heard you or understood you.

Case study 3.4

CONVEYING THE MESSAGE

Visitors returning from India said that they had found immense difficulty getting the meals they wanted in the house they rented. The staff had been told daily what was required and had all said 'Yes', with a nod and a smile.

But come the evening and the same meal was served day after day. However hard the visitors tried to explain they wanted something different, they still met with smiles and a 'yes'... and they still got something other than what they had ordered.

At a party they were complaining to some resident friends, who explained that the local culture was always to please guests. That meant avoiding any conflict, even at the level of questioning what was meant, or having to explain that what the visitors

▶

wanted was not available. Basically, the staff had not understood but had still seemed to agree, rather than give offence. The message simply had not been received so it could be acted on – although the words had been delivered by the visitors.

You may have stood in a foreign hotel, where the receptionist speaks no English. Up comes a British tourist and says something in English, which is received with a shrug of the shoulders, a quizzical smile and a shake of the head by the receptionist. One traditional approach for handling this problem is to repeat the same message, only much more loudly and a lot more slowly. In really sophisticated situations the tourist even adds a touch of the local accent, while still using their own language. Unfortunately, saying something unintelligible more loudly, slowly and in a funny accent does not make it easier to understand if it's in a foreign language. Communication has not taken place because for that to happen the message has to be received and understood.

So for communication to be effective, it requires a message, someone to receive the message and someone to receive it. Miss out any of those and communication doesn't happen. We all think we explain ourselves pretty well, but the receiving part of this – listening – is a very poorly applied skill. So when you are trying to make your point, never assume the other person has really listened to and heard what you're saying. This is as true in your own language as it is in someone else's. Just because you have uttered the words does not mean that they have been heard and can be acted on.

But it is not only other people. Virtually everyone can be a bad listener and this means you. If you want to state your own point of view, it is essential to know what the other viewpoint is, or you will go off at a tangent.

This means that the first thing you must do is to make sure that you have heard and understood what they really said – and that means listening, a key skill when it comes to handling yourself in these situations. Getting someone else to listen to you starts with you making sure you listen to and understand them and their point of view. But it can be hard. We all like to think we are good listeners but in truth most of us absorb only around 8 per cent of the words we hear.

Self-test 3.3

ARE YOU LISTENING?

- Think of a discussion you had at home or at work within the last few days where someone persuaded you to change your mind about something.
- Note down three points you made during the debate.
- Note down three points the other person made.

It was probably easier to remember what you said. Your own point of view in a debate is usually well-formed, so you can concentrate on the delivery. The other person's point of view may be new to you. That means it is vitally important to listen and absorb this new information before deciding how to respond.

Listening (and making sure the other person knows that you are listening) is the first key step of assertiveness. Linked with it are other forms of communication – especially non-verbal communication and body language. As hearing messages clearly is so crucial to assertive behaviour, we return to it in Chapter 4 and look at it in detail. You'll also find tips and tricks sprinkled throughout this book.

So for now, do you think you are a good listener? And don't say 'pardon?'.

Disagreeing or saying you don't know

Telling someone you disagree with them can be a traumatic experience. It shouldn't be. Everyone is entitled to their own opinion, but in some circumstances it can be difficult to express. This is where the issue of confidence and self-belief comes up.

You have probably been at a meeting at some time when the discussion went in a direction you didn't like. You felt like saying that you didn't agree, but took the least line of resistance and kept quiet – thinking that everyone else agreed and you were the odd one out.

Then someone said exactly what you had been thinking and got universal recognition – almost a round of applause. You were right all along, but failed to share your valuable opinion with the colleagues round the table.

Another variation on this theme is when you think you're the only person in the room who doesn't understand what's being said. Rather than look foolish you stay quiet – until someone else says they're lost and 75 per cent of the rest of the people mutter in agreement. You were not the only one who did not understand and not the only one who felt intimidated to say so.

Would you rather that your doctor made a guess at a diagnosis if they weren't sure, or would you prefer them to say they didn't know yet, but would find out with a few more tests?

Not knowing and not understanding is not a sign of failure or weakness. It's a fact, at times. Being able to say you don't understand or you don't know is a sign of maturity and strength.

Remember the key points in this checklist of your rights and responsibilities.

Checklist 3.1

YOUR RIGHTS AND RESPONSIBILITIES

I am entitled to ...

- Have an opinion of my own, even if it is different from other people's;
- Express my opinion and have it listened to;
- Say that I don't agree and expect others to listen with respect;
- Speak up if I need clarification or help to understand.

I have a responsibility to ...

- Recognise that others have these same rights;
- Share my own ideas and thoughts with others, rather than deprive them of what I know which may be helpful.

Take this situation where you disagree with someone in authority.

Self-test 3.4

DISAGREEING WITH THE BOSS

The chairman tells you the board plans to axe the junior management training programmes. You know the plan will cause ill feeling. Morale is already low. Do you:

(a) Say something – the board might not be aware of grassroots feelings? ❒

(b) Say nothing – you can't disagree with the chairman? ❒

(c) Go away meekly, but later send a memo? ❒

Whilst it may be easier for now to say nothing, it may not be the wisest decision in business terms. How would the chairman feel if, when the plan goes disastrously wrong, you said you knew it would but had kept quiet?

The bottom line, even if the chairman is someone who would ignore your observations if you made them at the time, is that they could never say you hadn't been honest at the time. Feeling uncomfortable about challenging the opinions of those in authority says more about the chairman than you. Only paranoid megalomaniacs will sack you simply for disagreeing – and do you want to work for one of them anyway? You are much more likely to be dismissed for sabotaging the chairman's plan in an attempt to prove you were right.

Ask yourself a few questions.

- What sorts of subjects do you (and don't you) feel comfortable discussing with senior management?

- Can you discuss them with some managers and not others?
- When you have to raise a tricky issue how do you prefer to tackle it?

This should give you some clues as to how easy you find it to handle this situation.

Disagreeing with people that work for you is easier. After all, aren't managers there to tell their team what to do and, if necessary, think? But beware! Imagine how you would feel in their shoes? Remember the thoughts you noted down about your relationship with your own boss and recognise that people often feel the same sorts of emotion. If you feel that way, assume they will, too.

An assertive approach to disagreeing with people means that you have to acknowledge both sides of the argument. So how do you rate? Is getting people to change their minds and listen to your view a problem for you? Do you find it hard to disagree?

5. Handling unexpected conflict

■ ■ ■

The severity of an unexpected problem often dictates the individual's decision to face it and fight or run for the hills. For a manager, the option of running isn't normally there. The effective manager, cornered like the proverbial rabbit in the head lights, cannot really take the first bus out of town! If an angry customer or another manager from a different department storms in with a serious complaint, you can't say you're not feeling very positive at the moment … could they come back later?

However, you might still roll over and submit. Rather than physically run, the passive response is to agree to anything that stops the conflict and gets the problem out of your face instantly. So you may have fled, metaphorically. Or you may have fought back, giving as good as you got, trading insult for insult and generally helping put out the fire by throwing more petrol on it.

Questionnaire 3.1 at the beginning of this chapter will have given you some idea as to whether your personal style is to confront (fight) or avoid (flee from) confrontation. The real issue here is the extent to which you were able to retain self-control and handle yourself and the situation with any degree of calm and logic. It is possible to overcome one's instinctive reactions with reason, but only if the desire to is great enough. So next you need to establish whether your reactions differ according to the sorts of conflict you face.

- Think of five instances where an unexpected conflict has made you angry, upset or frustrated.
- Now note down against each example why the conflict made you feel the way it did. What was the underlying issue that caused you to feel this way? What did you do that left you feeling like that? What did the other person do?

Your reactions are likely to be very varied – and they're unique to you. An angry reaction to a difficult situation could be sparked off by one of the following, for instance:

- you/your rights were being threatened;
- you felt physically and/or emotionally threatened by someone who wouldn't listen, who was intimidating and rude;
- the reaction triggered in you by the other person made you flare up and lose your cool and your self-control;
- you didn't respect the person confronting you;
- you felt impatient, because the problem was a recurrence of something you thought had been solved;
- you felt caught out, unprepared and off-guard;
- you were frustrated because the person bringing you the problem should have resolved it himself;
- it was the last straw in a long-term issue which could no longer be contained;
- you were camouflaging your own fear.

How do you rate at maintaining self-control in sudden and unexpected situations where there's potential conflict?

6. Preparing to handle a difficult situation

When you are faced with a potentially difficult situation how do you prepare to handle it? Do you prepare for it, or just go in hoping for the best, so they end up like the situations that arise without warning and you handle on the wing? Whenever possible it helps to prepare yourself first.

Unfortunately, knowing you have a nasty experience to face can make it grow bigger and less welcome as it gets nearer – maybe telling someone they are to be made redundant, discussing poor timekeeping or performance with an employee, or telling someone that what you promised to do has turned out to be impossible.

There are lots of different ways of preparing to handle a difficult situation – writing notes, posing questions, rehearsing the episode like a play, talking it through with a trusted friend or colleague (where appropriate). One manager even recorded herself on her dictaphone to see if she sounded convincing on not!

The main thing is to give yourself a chance to look at the situation objectively and anticipate the way the confrontation might go. You have to remember that you can't change the news you're going to give them. All you can do is break it sensitively. It also makes it possible to empathise without necessarily agreeing with what the other person says. Managers faced with having to make staff redundant, for example, can't change company decisions and let everyone keep their jobs; the redundancies have to be made. Empathising can help to calm down this extremely difficult situation and try to get something constructive out of the proceedings.

So, it's time to think through how you rate. Do you prepare properly for difficult situations or do you tend to busk it, and just see how it goes? Do you think through what you want to achieve, or leave it to chance and constantly get caught out?

One simple way of doing the diagnostic is to ask yourself questions about the way you usually behave.

Questionnaire 3.2

ANGER AND WHAT TO DO WITH IT

1 If someone criticises you, what do you normally do? Do you believe everything that person says and go into your shell, do you fight back with all your might? Or do you handle it more assertively and maturely by listening and then calmly responding?

2 If someone gets really angry with you what do you do? Do you fight anger with even greater anger? Do you curl up into a ball and give in?

3 What would you do if you felt really upset about the way someone behaved towards you at work? Would you say how upset you were and explain why to the person? Would you bottle it up?

Your answers to these simple questions are what can help you to find the areas you need to work on.

Where to now?

Hopefully, this chapter will have given you an insight into your personal style and the way you handle situations at the moment. It should also have given you some idea of the sorts of problems you would like to be able to handle more positively.

For each of the following give yourself a rating between one and ten. One would mean you have a great way to travel; towards ten and you are simply building on successful performance already. As before, be as honest as you can.

Questionnaire 3.3

MY PERFORMANCE AT THE MOMENT

1 *You and your manager* – how are relations, could they be improved?

2 *Saying 'No' (and 'Yes')* – faced with a difficult moment do you say 'Yes' when you should say 'No'?

3 *Conquering the fear of being disliked* – not easy, but are you happy not to be part of the gang sometimes?

4 *Stating your point of view* – how effective are you?

5 *Controlling yourself in difficult situations that flare up* – how well do you do this?

6 *Preparing to handle a difficult situation* – do you plan things through or leave things to chance?

And now ask yourself what areas you particularly want to work on as you go through the rest of this book, where we cover techniques you can use to build confidence and put your beliefs into practice.

It is time for the assertiveness window again.

Window 3

THE HIDDEN AGGRESSOR

Aggressive behaviour can take many different guises and come from the unlikeliest of sources. Normally passive people may express an aggressive side to their nature through covert actions which, at first glance, are not obviously aggressive.

George Brown, who was a manager for an insurance company, experienced this phenomenon first hand.

'A significant part of my job involved writing reports on insurance claims, part of the assessment procedure before agreeing a settlement. As a matter of course, these reports would be seen by Victor, my departmental manager. This should have been a rubber stamping exercise but my reports always came back covered in amendments – not just the odd comment but major editing. Even if you feel you are doing a good job, to get this sort of feedback constantly, without any real explanation as to why, is very demoralising. It turned out that everybody in the office had the same experience – in fact it was known as "the Victor effect"!

'Although Victor was usually quite a passive person, his comments on reports could be exceedingly vitriolic. When we challenged him we were simply told that he had been on an Open University course in business reporting – he knew what he was talking about. We came to the conclusion that Victor was simply venting his aggression in the safest way possible.'

So what was the solution to the problem?

'Eventually, we tackled the problem quite successfully. We held a departmental meeting to discuss how our reports could be improved. In the meeting we explained to Victor the sorts of comments we found helpful – and those we felt weren't constructive. It took some time but we did reach a consensus. From then on we held regular team meetings to discuss reports and share ideas as to how to improve them. It certainly improved the feedback we got from Victor (who hadn't realised his comments were that aggressive). But it also helped us all to learn from each other – we're a much better team now.'

4

Assertiveness – taking those first steps

Getting started

Now that you have explored the background to assertiveness it's time to look at the steps you can take to help yourself to become more assertive. In this chapter we are going to focus on a simple but incredibly powerful foundation for assertive behaviour. There are many more sophisticated techniques later in the book, but unless the first stages are covered, anything more clever won't work for you. In fact, if you do no more than apply the principles covered here, you will find situations starting to turn round for you.

But there is a problem. Only you can do it. Nobody else can change the way you act, so while we can explain the basics, it's down to you to try them out. Experience from running workshops and courses on the basics of assertiveness tells us that many people simply do not believe these simple stages will work as strongly as we claim. However, those who try them and develop them as second nature come back and confirm they do work – and work very well indeed. So try them – after all, what have you got to lose?

Don't think, though, that everything will happen at once. Assertiveness is an approach you can gradually build up and develop, and apply to more and more situations. It's like a muscle; the more you use it the better its condition and the greater the results. Don't think either that you need to become a kind of superhuman person able to deal with every situation all at once. It won't work that way.

So, where do we start from? Well, by confirming that assertiveness techniques do work, but work best if they are founded on values and beliefs that are in tune with the principles.

Understanding rights and responsibilities

We've already touched on this earlier but it really is a very crucial issue to remind yourself about. Underpinning the whole ethos of assertiveness is the idea that people need to acknowledge their own rights and responsibilities, and those of the people they're dealing with.

All too often human relations go wrong when people violate the rights of others and apply techniques without them coming from the heart. This can be quite simple. For instance, if your boss asks you in to hear your ideas and then interrupts you the whole time, he is saying one thing and doing another. If this happens, your boss is violating your right to have a say. The bottom line is that you know exactly what the real situation is; here's someone who says he listens, who is either deluding himself or is lying.

It is a painful possibility that you may well be a culprit of this kind of thing yourself. When was the last time you interrupted someone because you were too busy or not interested enough to listen to what they were saying?

The key here is to think through what people's rights and responsibilities are, and when you're clear about these you can then go on to use them as the bedrock of your assertiveness push.

So what do these rights actually look like? Well, everyone has a right:

- to be listened to,
- to be forgiven if they make a mistake, say the wrong thing, or generally demonstrate human fallibility,
- to say they don't know or they don't understand,
- to have their own set of beliefs,
- to be able to express those beliefs,
- to have feelings,
- to have and suggest ideas,
- to be treated fairly and not to be given all the horrible jobs,
- to be taken seriously and not to be harassed in the workplace.

Look back over this list and cross out any that you do not believe you are entitled to. Unless you are extraordinary, you will not have lifted your pen, as most of us feel that these are all examples of how we should expect to be treated. But rights bring responsibilities and the other side to the coin is that if you expect others to recognise your rights, you have a responsibility to treat them with respect, in return. So the next short step is to recognise that human beings all feel the same way.

Once you accept this then you can start interacting with people on a more even and fair and indeed grown-up footing. But all this is about principles and values – not about practicalities. Life isn't fair and you may not experience the benefits of these rights yourself, so why should you apply them in your dealings with others?

In practical terms, what does it mean for the way you interact with people, if you live by a code that recognises these rights and responsibilities? Some of the benefits of starting to look at the world in these terms are as follows:

- Listening to people can clarify that you were going to tell them things they already know. This can save time and avoid the danger of appearing patronising. You may even learn something new, from their experience and knowledge.

- Increased tolerance when people make mistakes increases the likelihood that they will ask for help and guidance before getting something wrong. If they do make a mistake, it is more likely to be turned into an opportunity for learning, to avoid it happening again.
- By hearing their view you could discover a new solution to the problem you're both trying to resolve – you don't have the sole rights to sensible answers and solutions.
- Understanding their beliefs and their situation might explain their behaviour – it may even make you think it was reasonable in the circumstances.
- If you let them express their beliefs and views, they'll be happier to hear your point of view later.
- By acknowledging their feelings, you increase the chances that they'll respect yours more ... everyone's human.
- Treat them fairly: they're likely to think you're a better manager and may accept compromise more willingly.
- Let them suggest ideas and they'll respect you for listening. Who knows, it could be that great award-winning idea you've been looking for!
- Take them seriously and they'll feel valued, perform better – and won't slag you off in the canteen/tell their colleagues how ghastly you are.

And remember:

- it's the most basic human right not to be harassed, treated unfairly or discriminated against in the workplace.

The right to be wrong

■ ■ ■

One of the things that often stops people from expressing their point of view is the fear of being wrong.

It's a habit we learn as young children. Perhaps from sitting in the classroom, not wanting to put our hand up in case we give the wrong answer to the teacher's question. Or simply from a parent telling us we're too young to really know what we're talking about.

Unfortunately, these childhood experiences tend to stay with us. While school often deals in right and wrong answers, management is more about judgement and balance, in a world where very little is clearly and obviously right or wrong. If it were, there would be no need for strategic discussion and decision-making.

Then teenage rebellion sets in. Suddenly we learn that we do have the right to say what we think. We may reject our parents' views as old fashioned and totally irrelevant, but never take the time to think whether our own views are really right.

Managers can't afford to carry on like rebellious teenagers. Storming out of meetings and threatening never to come back is aggressive and won't solve much! But managers do have the right to express their opinions, even if they do turn out to be wrong.

Saying nothing means no one will even think about your point of view – and just because you think you're wrong doesn't mean you are or that nothing useful will result from your thoughts. You may even be right. It is not unknown for someone to spot a basic flaw in an argument and prevent a disaster by speaking out in time. Most of us have been at meetings where someone quietly says, 'Why don't we do it this way', totally across the flow of what is being decided. The ensuing silence indicates that this individual has spotted something that everyone else has missed and, thankfully, has said so.

An assertive approach means you have the right and the responsibility to say something. You and your audience also have the right to accept that view is wrong after you've discussed it. Everyone wins.

Similarly, if the people working to you make the odd mistake, or say something that you feel is wrong, remember the old saying:

'Anyone who never made a mistake never made anything.'

As long as mistakes are used to learn from and not allowed to become an accepted part of the work process, there are even benefits in occasional cock-ups.

Where to now?

■ ■ ■

Having accepted that there's an issue of rights, what happens next? What are the practicalities? The aim of an assertive transaction is to reach a solution that, in descending order of desirability, either:

- suits everyone,
- is one that everyone can live with in the light of the real circumstances,
- is not what you want but at least has included your right to say your piece.

The third option is a great deal better than suffering in silence, but it is a very poor last choice. With proper use of techniques you should be able to achieve one of the first two, but to do this implies communication that flows between you and the other party, each having a say and in turn hearing what the other has to say. If either party is not listening, there can be no communication.

Break down the process of communication in a situation where you and the other person want different outcomes and you need to find some middle ground, and you can see it means that each of you has to have a say, be heard and look for a workable resolution.

Let's look at it as a simple ABC of assertiveness that works this way.

The assertiveness ABC

To achieve a reasonable result you have to:

- hear and acknowledge the other person's point of view,
- state your own views, feelings and opinions,
- agree a way forward.

If any of these components is missing, the situation will go wrong. There are three potential failure points.

1. Failing to hear their point of view means you are being aggressive – not taking account of their needs and feelings and denying them their rights.
2. Failing to state what you feel or believe means you are acting passively and giving in – holding back from exercising your rights.
3. Failing to identify a way forward is to miss the point of the whole exercise – to reach an outcome that works.

These three issues are reflected in the three stages in the ABC of assertiveness we are moving into. These are:

Actively listen – and show you're listening.

Be clear about your own views, feelings and beliefs.

Come to an agreed decision about what will work best in the circumstances.

Actively listen

If you believe that people have a right to be listened to then this is no problem. But even if you're not naturally a good listener there are very sound tactical reasons why you should aim to improve listening skills. Listening is crucial to achieving good results through assertiveness because:

- someone who sees that he has been listened to starts to calm down and is more prepared to listen in return;
- you cannot know exactly what his position is unless you hear it – all of it – and avoid jumping to conclusions half way through a sentence and interrupting once you've made the assumption that you know what's coming next. This can be remarkably dangerous, as this simple example from our own experience illustrates.

Case study 4.1

A LACK OF LISTENING

'I recently rang my bank to congratulate them on getting right a fairly complex transaction, with a high level of personal skill on their part. Admittedly, they simply did things like ring back when they said they would, send the right documents on time and keep me informed, but that was so unusual that I wanted to say "Thanks".

'When I rang to speak to the manager, I was asked what it was about. I said it was to comment on the way they had dealt with my transaction and I was told the manager was tied up, but would ring me back. Sure enough, he did, and as soon as I said I wanted to comment on the customer service he interrupted me. "Any complaints", he said, "are handled through our set procedure. Perhaps you would write in to me and I promise to look into it and respond within seven days?"

'All I wanted to do was give people a pat on the back, and what he heard was exactly the opposite, based on an assumption and a lack of listening. I still said what I rang to say, because it was the counter staff who deserved the accolades, but started to wonder whether the bank really did listen, as they claimed.'

It may seem unfair that you have to be the one who listens, when the other person seems incapable of doing so, but unless one of you stays calm and controls the process, it can escalate and turn into a quite heated conflict.

So you listen; you don't jump in, get angry, or try and say what you think before you've given other people a chance to speak. But listening is more than simply staying quiet and nodding. It means really hearing what they are saying, suspending your own feelings of resentment, fear or anger and trying to understand exactly what they are feeling and saying.

Active listening

At this stage, what you say and the actions you use must prove that you actually have listened to people, so they realise that you have concentrated, have heard them and are taking what they said seriously. This requires effort and thought; it needs you to respond carefully to what they are saying to you, rather than react emotionally.

Two subtly different ways of responding to show you're listening are:

- reflecting back to them what they have said, maybe paraphrasing or even just repeating it;
- acknowledging the underlying importance to them of their message.

On the other hand, the wrong thing to do is to react emotionally. Lose your temper and you lose control. If you need to, count to three before responding.

To illustrate the skills needed at this stage and in the other two, we'll follow a scenario through, where a deadline is changed by the customer. You are the production controller, and already working under considerable pressure.

Then your boss storms in and says:

> *'We have to get the Smithson job out by Friday. They've brought the deadlines forward, so drop everything and get on with it.'*

Your initial reaction may be absolute frustration; you've already altered schedules to fit in that job for the Doomes Foundation, so the temptation may be to utter a few well-chosen words that invite the boss to leave you alone. But, having maintained your self-control you could say – to show you have picked up the message clearly – either:

'The Smithson machines. By Friday?'

or

'Right. I can see that's a priority then.'

In neither case are you saying you can drop everything. You're just acknowledging in the clearest possible way that the message has been received and understood. And the message is not only that the deadlines have been changed, it is also that the boss is under pressure to get it sorted out. This second part of the message, hearing the boss's feelings, is a vital component in the listening process.

Getting your message across

The trouble is that there is already work in progress that you were told is also required for Friday and you don't have the capacity to do both, given the tight restrictions on payroll costs. Therefore, you can't just accept the instruction, because it will lead to greater problems later when you fail. The only option is to grasp the nettle and explain the real situation.

You don't apologise or make excuses, but you do say what you feel and believe, linking your confirmation of what they said to you with your own views. The most natural linking word is 'but'... and it can be dangerous!

'I can see that's a priority, BUT ...'

Work on the assumption that 'Yes, but' actually sounds like a hard 'No' to the listener. Try and avoid it at all costs. Instead use softer words and phrases that are less confrontational but still make the same point – such as:

- however ...
- on the other hand ...
- mind you ...

- unfortunately ...
- the trouble is that ...

Then add what you want to get across to the listening stage and the link.

> *'The Smithson machines by Friday? I can see that's a priority. The trouble is that I am already working on the Doomes order, as you instructed, and while I'd like to finish it all we can't get them both done with the present restrictions on overtime.'*

You have not argued, been rude or simply refused. All you have done is to add the second stage in the ABC to the listening stage. You have said only that you would like to do it (which is true), but it is physically impossible in the circumstances.

Interestingly, it is almost certain that the boss has already worked this out, and knows as well as you that it can't be done. It begs the question, why ask you in the first place? We don't know the answer to this – just that it happens. What we do know is that it will probably come as no surprise at all when you confirm the reality.

If the boss has already worked out that there is a problem, it could well be at this point that they ask simply, 'What the heck can we do, then?' This opens the door to the third stage, where you explore workable options. If they haven't worked it out, or seem unwilling to face reality, they may say something unrealistic in turn, such as:

> *'I don't want excuses. Just get it done.'*

But all the shouting in the world cannot change the laws of physics, so you have to stand your ground, calmly and logically. We looked at several examples of what happens when you give in to unrealistic demands, in earlier chapters, so the paramount importance of not fading into a passive approach will come as no surprise.

> *'I appreciate the problem and it's one I share, naturally. However, as much as I would like to say it can be done, I know that I would let you down with either Smithson's or Doomes if I said yes and I don't want that to happen. I'm sure you don't either.'*

This repetition of the message is a technique that we shall return to later, when we explore more sophisticated tools of assertive behaviour.

Finding a solution

So far you have used stages 1 and 2. You've listened and had your say. But what is the answer? That depends on the circumstances, of course, and there may simply be no way of getting the Smithson order out by Friday.

Mind you, it may be possible here – if the Smithson order is that crucial to the company strategy – to get dispensation on overtime. So you could say:

> *'We could do both if Finance would approve three hours overtime for ten staff each night for the rest of the week. Is that worth you pursuing?'*

If it is a possibility, it could solve at least part of the problem.

Knock-on effects

In this scenario, the boss should contact the customer anyway, whatever the outcome. If overtime is available, it still needs some thinking about in business terms. The knock-on effects must be considered and may require the boss to use the same ABC of assertiveness with Smithson's.

Even if overtime is not an option, you still deal with reality. It may turn out to be necessary for the boss to go back to Smithson's and explain it can't all be completed, maybe asking which parts of the order are essential by the weekend and which can follow next week. If all that fails, despite the fact that it is a difficult situation with Smithson's, it is still infinitely preferable to let them know now that there is a problem, rather than let them wait until it is too late. In terms of potential lost business:

- Waiting and letting them down would be almost guaranteed to destroy their faith in you as a supplier.
- A better option is to ring now to say despite your best efforts you know that their revised deadlines are impossible (bearing in

mind they changed them); you could though, agree to a revised schedule that is realistic and still better than the original.

- Negotiating which machines they need first is almost a positive move, as it demonstrates concern for their business and shows that you are not prepared to make promises you can't keep.
- Overtime gives Smithson's what they want … but is it the best option for you, in the long term? Will it lead them to believe they can mess you about in future? What effect does it have on costs?

In fact, even if overtime is an option, the most productive approach may be to ring Smithson's and offer them two alternatives … assertively, of course:

- the new deadlines at a renegotiated price to compensate you for the additional production costs, or
- the urgent parts of the order first, followed by less urgent parts next week.

So, the third stage of any assertive transaction is where you suggest a way forward. This means that assertiveness is about hard business success and not just about blurting out your feelings and listening to other people's points of view.

It's also more than just a simple talking shop. Assertiveness has a point which is to move towards a resolution that is likely to be based on compromise, on an understanding of other people's points of view and a practical no-nonsense approach to moving a difficult situation on.

This means that any assertive interaction will end with you helping to summarise and look forward to the next steps. This is important because it is the big bonus of assertiveness.

It's also why so many companies take assertiveness very seriously. They can see that there are real benefits because what it does is, it ends log jams, and ends what have sometimes been very difficult to solve problems, by suggesting that all-important way forward.

The ABC approach may sound simple ... and indeed it is. However, it does take practice and work to make it second nature. One common objection is that it must sound false and contrived, to use a formula like this. Based on experience and feedback from dozens of managers who have adopted the ABC approach, the reality is that it goes unnoticed by those on the receiving end.

So try it. It is by far the best chance you have of avoiding win–lose situations and developing a lot more win–win scenarios.

Language

The words and phrases you use carry important messages about whether you're assertive, passive or aggressive. In any assertive transaction there are words and phrases that are positive. We've looked at some examples, like alternatives to the word 'but'.

Two other very powerful words in assertiveness are 'yes' and 'no'. Saying 'Yes' tends to surprise people, especially if they are expecting a battle. It is very helpful in confirming that you have listened and it opens the door for them to listen to you.

'No' is harder. It is an under-used word, especially by passive individuals who hate the feeling that someone will be offended if they say no. If this rings bells with you, find alternatives that sound less harsh, like:

– *'I'm afraid not'.*

– *'Unfortunately that's impossible'.*

We're not going to list dozens of alternatives here because you don't need us to tell you how to use simple language. All that really matters is that it isn't only what you say, it is equally how you say it. Nobody minds 'Yes', whereas 'No' and 'But' are harder to handle ... so work round them. As long as the message is clear and you can make your point clearly, you don't have to be seen to be dogmatic.

Passive language

Indicators of passivity come through some of the words and phrases used. Try to avoid – or at least to limit – words and phrases that tell other people that you are passive from the start, such as the following, which are just a few examples.

- *'I'm sorry …'* (if you're not, why say you are?);
- *'I'm sure I'm wrong but …'* (if you're sure you're wrong, why are you saying anything?);
- *'I know it's trivial …'* (when what you really mean is, the person you're talking to may think it's trivial, but actually it isn't).

Aggressive language

Aggressive people ignore the rights of others. In many situations aggressive language is obvious, angry and even abusive. On other occasions the speaker may mean no harm and come out with comments like:

- *'What you need to do is …'*
- *'That's stupid …'*
- *'Oh, come on!'*

Again, we neither can, nor do we intend, to try to list a great deal here. What matters is that you think about the words and phrases that convey aggression.

In addition, sexist, racist or any other discriminatory comments are aggressive. The speaker is likely to defend their statements by saying that those on the receiving end can't take a joke, but if it gives offence it is aggressive. Saying, 'I didn't mean to hurt you', after the event, confirms they were hurt.

Included here are patronising remarks, or comments that deride or sneer at any individual or group, or pat them on the head as a way of ignoring their feelings and views. In many situations the person acting in such a patronising way does not realise the effects of their actions but, for instance, treating a secretary or a front-line machine operator as some form of unintelligent and unfeeling lower order on the evolutionary scale is to deny them basic human rights. Any actions or words based on assumptions, stereotypes and personal prejudice are a flaw in management performance and are signs of aggressive behaviour.

The only way to look at this sort of issue is to put yourself in the shoes of other individuals and groups and see how it feels. The chances are that it has happened to you when you were starting out in a career, so you know what it felt like then. It still feels like that now, for those affected.

Body language

The words you utter convey a great deal of meaning. They also say a lot about you as a person, your values, beliefs and natural approach to handling situations. However, your tone of voice conveys far more clearly whether you are aggressive, passive or assertive.

Tone

This is a clear area where what is said is less important than how it's said. Hesitant speech, littered with frequent 'umms' and 'errrs' is often a sign or passivity or a lack of confidence. Another indicator can be a tone that drifts upwards uncertainly towards the end of every sentence as if every statement is there to be challenged.

On the other hand, loud and fast conversation, delivered like bullets from a gun, generally marks out someone who wants to get their comments in over anyone else. Someone who interrupts all the time, or won't stop talking may also demonstrate aggressive speech patterns, as may the individual who drops their tone on the last word or two, making it hard to question any of their statements.

An assertive tone is friendly, factual, confident and clear. It neither threatens nor apologises, is well paced and calm.

Let's take two examples – uncertainty and sarcasm – to explore in a bit more detail what effect tone can have on a message.

Imagine you ask a passive employee whether they're confident they can do a job for you and they say 'Yes', but with a slight tremble in their voice and a sort of question mark running through it. What does it tell you? It says they aren't sure. They said 'Yes' but they didn't really mean it, probably because they didn't like to say 'No', but hoped you would spot the signals and pursue the question. If an aggressive manager takes the word at face value, they would leave the employee to it and almost certainly return to find they'd failed. No winners here.

On the other hand, an assertive manager picking up the real message from the uncertain tone and saying something like, 'You don't sound too sure', gives them the opening they need to explain what is giving them cause for concern.

Sarcasm is particularly aggressive and suffers from the disadvantage that what one person finds funny is seen as downright insulting by another. It's often a way of scoring points off someone else at their expense. Get someone to tell you they think you're a great manager, in a really sarcastic tone, and see how it feels.

Physical signs and signals

Other aspects of body language centre on physical appearance, gestures, posture and facial expressions.

Many managers will have had the gruelling experience of a video training session. Unless you have hidden talents and are a budding Richard Burton, there is nothing quite as awful as watching yourself give a presentation or conduct an interview!

Whilst these training sessions are gruesome, they do highlight an important aspect of communication – body language. According to recent research done by Kodak the visual impression someone makes accounts for 55 per cent of the information we take on board from that individual.

If you are the kind of person that goes through life with either passive or aggressive body language then you have room for improvement. One difficulty can be that, unless you have had the uncomfortable benefit of being on video, you may not be aware of how you come across to others.

These are just a few examples of how aggressive and passive body language look to other people on the outside.

Checklist 4.1

BODY LANGUAGE

Aggressive people may display the following characteristics, among others.

Body	Invading your space, leaning forward or over you and often wagging a finger at you or standing while you have to sit.
Head	Their head very close to yours, making you feel uncomfortable, sometimes with the head thrust forward of the neck, like a sort of probe.
Eyes	Staring, wide and glaring … or with the eyebrows furrowed in an angry way, often coupled with excessive eye contact to the point where you feel as if you are being examined under a light.
Face	Granite-like, impassive, slightly screwed up.
Voice	Either very loud or very soft and, if it's soft, measured in the way the words come out.

Passive people often show the following signals, among many others.

Body	Hunched, almost cowering, with some wringing of the hands, or perspiration, and/or fingering a collar.
Head	Pointing down, or turned away slightly.
Eyes	Looking down, blinking frequently or unable to make eye contact.
Face	A fixed smile or sickly grin, even when distressed.
Voice	Hesitant, maybe a bit trembly and trailing off.

The above signals are very hard to change, but they are worth working on if you are naturally either passive or aggressive. If you want to say assertive things you have to back them up with appropriate non-verbal messages.

Checklist 4.2

ASSERTIVE BODY LANGUAGE

There is no 'right' body language, but there are clusters that imply assertiveness. The sort of body language to aim for could include:

- Steady eye contact, without staring the opposition out.
- Standing with one's head held up.
- Sitting upright – neither looming forward nor slouching, with the soles of both feet on the floor and maybe the palms of the hands on the desk or table.
- A relaxed yet steady and firm jaw and mouth, with no signs of tension around the jaw or neck muscles.
- Looking comfortable and relaxed without losing posture and poise.
- Smiles, nods and frowns at appropriate places.
- Hand movements at a measured speed – not waving about frenetically.

So how do you know what signals you convey? The next time you have the chance, brief a friend of colleague (from whom you don't mind receiving frank feedback) to tell you what they think. Discuss with them what sort of non-verbal signals convey aggression, passivity and assertiveness, using the details you have just looked at. Then ask them to watch you closely the next time you are in a meeting together, or at home when you are handling a problem with the builder/decorator/shop assistant.

Try to get them to give you specific and detailed feedback on what they observed, and what message they picked up. It's also useful for them to monitor how other people seem to respond to your body language, as a further indicator of the effect you are having.

If you can't do this try to jot down a few notes immediately after you have dealt with a problem. Think about each element in turn and see if you can remember how the other person reacted to you.

Putting the ABC into action

■ ■ ■

For the rest of this chapter, we'll look at using the ABC approach in three situations that most of us have problems with:

- dealing with a difficult staff member,
- dealing with your boss,
- dealing with your colleague,

Let's start with the staff member.

Case study 4.2

WORK NOT DONE – THE STAFF MEMBER

You've had a really important order for one of your best customers that needs to be done by 5.30 p.m. on a particular day. In the morning, you spoke to the supervisor responsible who assured you that the order would be done. No problem. You checked again at lunchtime, and were assured again that everything was OK. The next morning you arrive to work at 8.30 a.m. to find the telephone ringing, and a very irate customer. The work wasn't done and the order wasn't delivered. This customer is now threatening to take his business elsewhere. What do you do?

You may well have come across this, and it's particularly annoying. Before looking at the assertive option, let's check on the other, less constructive approaches. You've got a number of other options, two of which are to act in the fight or flight manner we looked at earlier.

On the fight side, you have the option to storm into your staff member's office and give him a verbal pasting. This would not change this situation for the customer and would leave you and the staff member feeling angry and upset – at least for the rest of the day. As a row rarely sorts out the real roots of a problem, you would generate more heat than light, and leave a damaged relationship in the workplace that would be hard to repair.

Or you can simply avoid the problem and try to do the work yourself before the member of staff comes in. That way you don't have to create any waves. In this case you would bottle up your emotions and just feel resentful. You might even lie, telling the customer that everything will be ready in a couple of hours, when you know very well it won't be.

Given that neither of these options is appropriate, how can one actually use the ABC approach above to help the situation resolve itself?

For a start, it's important not to jump in and panic or lose control. You need to listen to what the staff member had to say. After all, there may well have been a very good reason why the order wasn't actually delivered on time. Then, when you've listened, you can actually do something about it.

Imagine then that when you talk to the staff member he has no real explanation for what's happened, other than the fact that he got very busy in the afternoon. What happens next?

Self test 4.1

SOMETHING TO THINK ABOUT ...

Think about the ABC approach and what you might say assertively in the above situation. You want to get across your feelings and you need to explain the difficulty this puts the company in. You also need to work out a way forward.

If you want to, make a few notes somewhere. But whatever you do, imagine the scene unfolding and hold a mental conversation that covers the ABC points.

This is where you can start to use some of the ideas from earlier in the chapter. There are no right or wrong answers, although the key points all need to be covered. So you might say something like:

> *'I've listened to what you say and I appreciate you did get very busy during the day.'*

This is important because you haven't forgiven the person or caved in. You've simply acknowledged that you did actually listen to them.

It's the first stage in that important dialogue you're hoping to get going. But what next?

What about this?

'However, although I know you had a problem, I'm very disappointed that you didn't tell me that it was developing during the day. You did know that this was an important order. So I do feel let down that you didn't let me know what was happening. What's more this has put the whole company in a very difficult situation with this important customer.'

Here you're stating very clearly and honestly how you feel about the situation and what it actually has meant to you. You haven't ducked away from giving the bad news, but you've actually said this causes a problem and that you're not happy.

And what next? Well it's a case of going on to Stage C – a way forward. Here are a few options that might fit.

First, if the customer is one you know well, and who has been in contact with the supervisor, you may decide to deal with it this way.

'We must discuss later what happened yesterday and look for ways to make sure it doesn't happen again. However, our main priority at the moment is to get that order done. So, I'd like you to go back, phone the customer and tell them honestly when they can expect to receive their order. Apologise if you need to, but don't lie; tell them what happened. The main thing is we need to get the order done. If there's anything I can do to help, please tell me.'

Or, if you have a particularly good relationship with the customer, it may be appropriate to say something like this.

'I need to ring the customer and explain. However, I shall give them a firm promise on when they can expect delivery. You and I should now agree a guaranteed time by which you'll have finished. We'll talk about yesterday's difficulties later, and look for ways to stop it happening again.'

Whatever fits the bill, you are looking for a solution that is acceptable on both sides. So you haven't shouted 'Get it done by 11.30' and stormed out, because that may not be practical. And anyway, it shows you sliding towards aggressive behaviour and another losing situation.

In this example you have acted as a calm and responsible manager and achieved the best result possible from a poor situation by:

- showing you listen,
- saying what you think and feel,
- agreeing a way forward.

To begin with, you listened and respected the person's right to have a view, and then their right to tell their side of the story – even though it was a pretty lame excuse. You then asserted the way that you felt and told them clearly what the issues were. Finally, you rounded up and got the assertive bonus. You kept your own blood pressure low. Hopefully, you'll be able to satisfy the customer, and you gave a clear plan of action to move forward.

All this sounds good, but it's easier maybe to handle someone when you have more authority than they do. What about dealing with your boss?

It might seem that it is a little bit more tricky to use the ABC approach. Well, try this one.

Case study 4.3

THE BOSS

You've had a long-standing meeting in Birmingham with one of your important customers. You've booked the ticket and not only are you looking forward to going, you think it's very important that you're there in order to secure more business. It's Thursday morning and you need to catch the train at 11.30 a.m. You're feeling quite tired because you already worked three late nights and really you just want to get going. First thing in the morning your boss comes in and tells you that she must have a report from you, on her desk by midday. She needs it for her own report that has to go to the board by the end of the day. What do you do?

Clearly again you've got a number of options.

You could say 'Yes' to the boss, although you've got no chance of sensibly doing it. This would lead to everyone being disappointed.

You could get very angry and shout at the boss. After all, you are tired, you have worked three nights late. The trouble is, the boss will shout back and just insist you do it, so that won't work and will only sour relationships.

This is a common dilemma. What do you do when you seem to have too much to do and your boss is being unreasonable?

The important thing is to go back to think about rights. Clearly, you have rights in this situation; your company and your boss have a responsibility to you, as a staff member as well. On the other hand, you have a responsibility to explain what is possible to the boss, and to allow her her own rights.

So, let's try the ABC approach again.

The first thing to do is to listen to the boss. So you might ask a question to find out why the report is so important. Assuming that you get a sensible answer, you then start to go into the next stage which is actually putting your own view.

So you might say something like this.

> *'I understand that the report is important. However, I have had this meeting booked in Birmingham for a very long time, as you know. We agreed last week that it's an important meeting and you did say you particularly wanted me to go because they seem to trust me. Cancelling will cause us quite a lot of problems with the client, and that may lose us some work.'*

You've clearly put your case, explained the facts of the situation and told your boss how you feel about it. You've even reminded her what her views and feelings are … or were when you discussed the meeting in Birmingham last week. You've also set out some of the main issues clearly and without getting angry.

There's an interesting side issue here, around whether the boss gets angry at this point. If she does, the question is whether she appears angry with you for telling the truth, or with whoever put her on the spot and asked for a last minute report for the board. In all probability she is really angry with herself, for not resisting the pressure for a late report or for having left things to the last minute.

All you are doing is reminding her of the facts of the situation, and expressing your views calmly. If that causes an adverse reaction, keep reminding yourself that you didn't cause the problem, but you are trying to help find a solution. Keep reminding yourself too that 99.9 per cent of humans (bosses included) are really pleasant and ordinary people who do their best in difficult situations. They're not ogres and what your assertiveness does is simply to make them face harsh realities. That's uncomfortable, but it does pass. In many cases like this, when any boss calms down enough to accept reality, their reaction is likely to be something like, 'Yes. I know you're right. What on earth are we going to do?'

On that note it's time to move to some kind of resolution. You may be able to make a suggestion to your boss something along these lines.

> *'Ultimately this is your decision, of course, and as I can't do both I need to know which is more important. But we do have some options here. I can go to Birmingham as planned, and get the report on your desk by midday tomorrow. Or we could ring them see about rescheduling the meeting. Or I could go to Birmingham if I were to get the basic facts together for you rather than write a full report. I suggest we look at the options and the implications together, before deciding. What do you think?'*

Again, this is an important example because it shows the way you can actually have your say, assert your rights, and get that all important assertiveness bonus at the end which is a resolution. A way forward without losing your cool or your self-control.

Dealing with colleagues

■ ■ ■

Dealing with colleagues can be equally difficult. One of the issues here you have is that if he has no line manager responsibility, it can be sometimes difficult to get your view heard.

The business of rank can be quite messy and sometimes people feel very prickly.

The following is an example of what can happen in these relations between colleagues and how an assertive response can actually help you.

Case study 4.4

BETWEEN COLLEAGUES

You work for a large retail institution in the marketing department. Your job in the brand services section is to establish solid guidelines for the way company products are going to look – consistent type styles, colours, etc.

You've been charged to do this job by one of the directors of the company and you're mid-way through drawing up a manual which specifies firmly the house-style people must stick to. It is a bit of a thankless job because many people outside marketing sometimes see this as unnecessary interference in their work.

People do have difficulty in understanding why brands are so important and you have tended to be cast as the villain of the piece. This sometimes makes it difficult in meetings, where it's hard for you to be liked, as people see you as simply interfering and always saying 'No'.

In this particular meeting, you're meeting up with some sales folk who want to actually design a new brochure. You've told them the way the project is going to develop brand standards and that it will have implications for the cover. Suddenly, someone turns on you. 'Listen. We're really sick of all this meddling on your part. Who do you think you are? The Gestapo?' The room dissolves into laughs as you sit in your chair with all eyes staring on you. What do you do?

Again, clearly you have a whole range of different options and there are some quite unpalatable ones.

You could simply lose your cool. Some people have been known to burst into tears in this kind of situation. After all, it's never very nice to be thought of as a stick-in-the-mud.

Or you could go on the attack. You could fight fire with fire and make a sarcastic comment in return. The difficulty with this is that it wouldn't solve anything, and it probably would lead to more trouble, with inter-departmental relations breaking down entirely in the future.

You could try to wheedle out of things by saying it isn't your fault. For instance you could say, 'Well it's not really my fault; the directors have told me to do this.' But that would be a kind of childlike excuse, or emotional blackmail. It is a manipulative kind of response and it fails to meet the standards of the ABC approach.

The only solution here is to behave like a grown-up and to behave assertively. So, how would it work?

Self test 4.2

SOMETHING ELSE TO THINK ABOUT ...

Think about the ABC approach and what you might say assertively. You want to get across your feelings and you need to explain why you do what you do. You also need to work out a way forward that will remove at least some of the problems and misunderstandings in future.

If you want to, make a few notes somewhere. But whatever you do, imagine the scene unfolding and hold a mental conversation that covers the ABC points.

The first stage is to acknowledge that you've listened to people. You then need to put your own view. So you might say something like this:

> *'OK, I hear what you say. I understand that it does seem as if we're being unduly pernickety about the brand standards. However, it's important for me to say that we aren't trying to stop your productivity. The reason we're doing this is that it's very important that every brand is seen from outside the company as part of the company. I understand your concerns about staff creativity, but we aren't actually trying to do that. There's plenty of room for that in terms of the way you write the material.'*

The next step. This is important because what you've done is acknowledged the people's feelings but you've clearly stated your own position and your own feelings. Indeed, you might add something like:

'I don't think it's very productive for us to get in to this state of warfare like this and to be firing off comments at each other. It's important that we do keep our heads and manage this discussion in a way that's going to help us move forward.'

After you've done this, the next stage is to suggest a way forward. You might do something like this:

'What I can do is take some of your concerns back to the committee I'm working with. However, it's important to say that we do need to move forward on this so what I'm suggesting is that I come back to you in two weeks' time when I've got fully made up versions of what the covers would look like, and I can show you the covers to try to allay your fears and show that they actually will serve your purposes. In the meantime, if you want to speak to me about any suggestions or areas where we could improve things, please do so. I'm always available to talk.'

This is a model because of what it does; it acknowledges people's feelings and gives them a sense that they have a stake in the way in which the project is moving forward. It also has been done with good humour and good grace and with fairness towards those involved. A by-product is that it may actually help stop people in the future behaving in a rather childish and almost school-playground way of sniping and firing off comments to each other.

We've taken you through some very basic ideas, and of course you will look in much more detail at different situations, but it should help you early on to start thinking through how you would handle difficult situations. It also shows how the simple three-stage approach can really help.

Getting started

So you've worked through some simple ideas about getting assertiveness started and through some of the basic ideas behind it. You've also examined a very basic ABC of assertiveness that can help in many different situations.

The next thing is for you to actually get out and start practising. It isn't easy but it's important to take the jump.

The following short checklist gives just some areas in which it can start to work in order to actually to get the ball rolling. So get out from behind your desk, close the door on your office and get out and do the following:

Checklist 4.3

BEING ASSERTIVE

- Start to say 'No' when you mean 'No'.
- Offer a way forward when you've been discussing difficult situations.
- Give praise when it's needed.
- Accept praise when it's given.
- Learn to listen and take on board people's comments before you jump in.

You might choose to take each element of the checklist in turn and try to introduce this approach into your working day or indeed you can just do which one you feel like doing. Let's look at each point and see how other managers have tackled these issues.

Saying 'No'

■ ■ ■

Enormous problems can arise from failing to say 'No' when it's necessary. When you're brave enough to say what you mean it can pay great dividends.

Case study 4.5

COPING WITH TOO MUCH WORK

Alison was a PA for a busy advertising agency. Her boss had a habit of dumping work on her. If the work didn't get done the boss yelled at Alison. So, unwisely, she ended up doing everything.

After a couple of months Alison could stand it no longer and decided to say something. The next time her boss tried to give her more work than she could cope with she said 'No'. He was stunned – but she managed to keep him talking. She explained what she was working on and asked what he felt could be postponed. By the end of the discussion they had decided which work was really urgent. Her boss had also promised to give Alison more support with her work. The next week she got an assistant.

120

Offering solutions to difficult situations

■ ■ ■

Sometimes there appears to be no way forward in a difficult situation. Fail to find a workable solution and in the end it will probably cost the company time, money and a great deal of heartache. It's all about compromise and about win–win.

Case study 4.6

WE NEED A LIBRARIAN

An editor at a large public body was placed in an impossible position when his two managers refused to agree on what his job should involve.

The problem was that the organisation needed a librarian and needed one badly. The task was slipped into the editor's job description in the hopes that he would cope with the added work load. After six months it became clear that this was a hopeless arrangement.

The two managers met to discuss the problem but quickly reached stalemate. One manager thought the editor should just

▶

be an editor, the other thought he was tailor-made to just be a librarian.

A compromise was found when the editor joined the meeting. He didn't really want to be a librarian, it didn't really feel right for him, but he could see someone had to do it. He suggested that he spend one day a week being official librarian, provided he could delegate another part of this job to a colleague. He could also move his desk into the library so he could help with any passing enquiries during the rest of the week. Perhaps not the perfect solution but at least it was a workable compromise. It was win–win.

Giving praise

■ ■ ■

Telling someone they have done a good job is one of the simplest and most effective ways of getting the best out of your staff. Given that it is so powerful it is amazing so few people do it.

Case study 4.7

PRAISE BE!

Sue was a junior valuer in the doll department at Christie's Auctioneers.

'Right from the first day junior valuers deal with clients face-to-face. To begin with, you ask the head of department what each piece is and what it's worth. The next time it's up to you to recognise the piece and tell the client yourself. It's how you learn – but it's easy to get despondent when you forget things.'

Sue's boss had the ideal remedy for this.

'Every time I got a valuation right, Olivia told me what a good job I'd done. In fact, she always said well done and thank you for any task that I completed successfully. It made me feel I was achieving something and try even harder the next time. It meant that when Olivia did tell me I'd got something wrong, or wanted something done differently, I was happy to accept it as positive feedback, not negative criticism. She taught me one of the best management lessons I ever learnt.'

Accepting praise

■ ■ ■

Inexplicably, lots of people find it hard to accept praise. It's embarrassing; perhaps it means the opposite of what's being said. The problem is that by not accepting praise gracefully you will probably make the person praising you think twice about doing it next time. It could be what motivated this manager's boss to behave as he did.

Case study 4.8

THE MANAGER'S STORY

'I had been really up-tight with my departmental boss for some time. I felt he didn't give my team or me any credit and basically got all the glory himself.

'One day we were talking at lunch and he said something about how he had improved production targets. I snapped a little. I told him in no uncertain terms that we all played a part in the success and that I felt unhappy with the way he presented and represented our contribution. It was a little heated but it really cleared the air.

'It turned out that he did sing our praises to his boss and did appreciate our work ... but just never told us because he thought we'd be embarrassed.'

Listen first; react after

■ ■ ■

When a good idea comes up it's hard not to react to it in the euphoria of the moment. On the flip side, people can jump in and crush an idea too quickly because they think it is daft or won't work.

Case study 4.9

RESEARCHING RESEARCHING

The research department of a major American university was running out of funds. An emergency meeting held to discuss the problem turned up the usual ideas – ask a benefactor to help or sell some ground-breaking research to a major corporation.

Soon after, the department's professor was studying electron microscope projections of cell tissue when his secretary commented that they looked like fabric designs for aerobics clothing. A brilliant idea! There's no copyright on nature's creations so maybe he could sell the images to a clothing company and raise some funds.

Luckily, the professor took time to discuss the idea with his colleagues. One of them asked why they needed to sell the images – his daughter was a designer and she made far more money from the designs she licensed. Which is exactly what they did. Today, the research department has a multi-million dollar licensing agreement with a top sports clothing firm and is entirely self-funding.

So that's it. You're on the road to assertiveness.

In the next section, we're going to look at an important area where assertiveness plays a crucial role, namely, effective negotiation.

Window 4

MIRACLES INVOLVE MORE STRESS

'I have a tendency to be a passive person – I want to do the best job possible and I don't like letting people down, even if it's not really my fault.

'A couple of instances come to mind. The first was a piece of work I did for the Health & Safety Executive. The project was running to a very tight deadline. We agreed a sensible schedule right at the start and everyone was happy with it. The problems started when I didn't receive some important information from the HSE on time. Eventually it came through, but by that stage I had other work waiting to be done; this caused a backlog and a real problem. The deadline was looming, but I didn't really want to go back on my promise. I went through hell working late into the night and worrying myself sick that I'd never make the deadline. I achieved a miracle and met the deadline but I was a stressed out wreck by the end of the process.

'The next time we worked together I decided to speak out right at the start. I explained that the late arrival of information from them had a knock on effect and made it very hard for me to produce work to agreed deadlines. The HSE seemed sympathetic. They obviously took my comments to heart. The next time they sent something through late it had a note attached saying that they realised the deadline would slip – when could I manage to do the work by?

'It's an experience that has taught me to be up front with people. Recently, I inadvertently double-booked myself to run the first of a series of ten management training days. I remembered my experience with the HSE and took the bull by the horns. I spoke to the client, admitted my mistake and asked if he had any suggestions as to how to solve the problem. "It's no problem," he said, "We'll just move the course back one week".'

5

Negotiating – a skill for all seasons

In this chapter we link assertiveness to one of the wider aspects of a manager's role at work. The topic is negotiation – a word that is almost as misunderstood as assertiveness itself.

Although people may not be clear about the word *negotiation* the truth is that the skills are invaluable in a whole range of situations at work and indeed in life too.

The caveman's common approach to difficult negotiations was to beat the opposition over the head with a large club. By the eighteenth century things had improved a bit – they would resort to sabres or pistols at dawn in a secluded field. Neither was the most constructive approach to solving a tricky situation.

Fortunately today's manager tends to approach negotiations in a rather more constructive manner. Negotiations are not so much about winning and losing but about reaching a sensible solution – preferably a win–win scenario. We live in the age of mediation and the search for common interest.

It can be a fraught process. Some people choose to solve these disputes swiftly and simply. Take this legendary example:

Case study 5.1

A COINED SOLUTION

Ayrton Senna chose a radical (but time-honoured) approach to negotiate his driving fee with McLaren team manager Ron Dennis. Stuck in a stalemate situation with a considerable difference between the fee each was willing to accept, they tossed a coin. Ron Dennis got lucky. He saved £2 million.

Generally, managers cannot afford to adopt such rash tactics. There are many different ways to handle negotiations. The important thing is that the manager achieves the result they and their organisation need.

Think about negotiations you have been involved in lately – anything from persuading your team to work longer hours to fixing terms for a deal with another company. Did you achieve what you wanted to? Which party came off best? When you disputed a point what approach made you agree to change your mind?

If you feel that you tend to achieve less than you would wish from negotiations, being more assertive could help you to achieve more. Negotiations also have their aftermath. If you're often manoeuvred into a losing position, your morale, not to mention your reputation, may suffer. On the other hand, if winning is the only option, do you find yourself doing anything to win?

The following is just a snapshot of the kind of areas in which negotiation skills are likely to come in handy. And it's just that – a snapshot.

So negotiation helps when you are called on to agree things like:

- work and performance targets,
- pay and conditions,
- conditions of service,
- what you and other managers will do on a project,
- when and how things are to be done,

- workplace norms: what time you need to show up to work, what you wear, how you behave in the workplace, what you call people.

Negotiation is part of the day-to-day transactions of life. Everyone negotiates on occasions. It is unlikely that you will ever end up in big 'set-piece' negotiations, but the same principles that apply there are appropriate at negotiations you will carry out. Changing workloads, agreeing budgets, accepting deadlines for work, altering staffing arrangements are just a few further likely examples.

The reason that negotiation is in a book on assertiveness is that it follows the same basic outline and has a common set of characteristics. The main difference is scale. Assertiveness is a personal approach where you listen, say what you think and aim for an agreement. Negotiation is structured and may involve teams of people … but it has the same ABC steps. So it is an interesting parallel. But it's also a situation where personal assertiveness can help bring negotiations to a positive conclusion more swiftly and with better outcomes.

What is negotiation?

■ ■ ■

We can see it in two contexts – at two levels.

In this book we are looking at negotiating as a skill for everyone, a process that we all use from time to time so we end up with an outcome that suits us … or that we can at least live with. At this level it is still extremely important and everyone benefits from being better at it. But most of us will never go – or want to go – on a two-week course in negotiation because it is not as important to us as other parts of our jobs and our lives.

However, there are people who do nothing but negotiate and there are books written solely for them, on negotiating as an expert topic. In this context it is a very specialist skill – almost an art form, and people who do it for a living tend to work in the industrial relations world, or in high-level selling, where the product is very expensive systems or equipment. Often there are many factors to be considered in negotiations at that level – for instance if someone is negotiating a pay deal affecting all the workers in an entire industry, or doing a multi-million pound deal for a power plant abroad.

In situations like these there are wide and often political factors involved. They might need to look at balancing job security against a short-term pay rise, or trade off some basic pay for increased holidays. Or it could be important to look at what proportion of local people get jobs, compared to expatriate people, or what other trade implications follow from such a major deal.

If you read those specialist books you will see a distinction drawn between negotiating and bargaining because it's especially important to differentiate when you work in that rarefied atmosphere. We don't need to cover all the ground those specialist texts do, but it does pay to look at where basic points can be lifted from the principles of major negotiations and applied to everyday work. It can help us get our own negotiations right, even in normal management situations.

Mutual interests and trade-offs

Negotiation is about finding common ground between people with different interests, meeting the overriding need to come up with a solution that is in the common interest.

So if you are involved in negotiating a delivery date, all you want to achieve is a date that suits you and the person you're delivering to. It's a question of trying different paths until you reach the one that gives you what you both want. You suggest one date, realise it doesn't suit them, see what else you can suggest. You discuss the reality of the situation quite openly as you're both aiming to find an answer that meets your common interest – which is that they get the goods when they need them. It is in their interests because they have to use the goods to sell on and fill their own orders, and it's in your interest because you want them to be satisfied customers, and come back with more orders.

Bargaining often plays a part in negotiations, and is generally about the price of something, whether it's the price of a car or the price of employing someone. It starts with a formal offer, then counter-offers until a resolution is reached. This involves trade-offs and concessions; 'We'll work an extra hour if you give us more money', or 'I can give you more money if you drop this other request'. The confusing part of this is that it's hard to know where bargaining ends and negotiation starts, as bargaining often includes periods of negotiation, and some day-to-day negotiation in turn includes bits of bargaining. For our purposes, though, see negotiation as the wider framework, with bargaining as one component, the trade-off element and the business of offers and counter-offers.

In the example of negotiating the delivery of goods, bargaining would be about saying, 'We can get them there on Tuesday, but it will cost you more for express delivery'. In the following example though, there are no trade-offs, just negotiation towards everyone's solution.

Case study 5.2

WE CAN DO IT TOGETHER

A small plastics factory in Scotland wanted to use some waste land it owned alongside the factory to build a small storage area. The trouble was that the construction process could interfere with deliveries in and out, unless it was carefully planned.

So the company's managers sat down with the builders to negotiate how to avoid slowing down the building work, while keeping deliveries going.

They agreed that the route to the delivery bay should go round the other side of the factory while building was in progress – an idea that came from the construction company. They also said that deliveries of building materials should be specified to arrive between ten and 11 in the morning, or three and four in the afternoon, and the construction company would write this into the terms they worked out with their suppliers. This would leave clear spaces for the plastics firm to receive and send out its own delivery vehicles, at different times.

They all realised afterwards that, while they had negotiated the way forward, they had worked together constructively to find solutions that suited them all. Each side had to make accommodations, but neither side had to make any real concessions to the other.

So negotiation is the process of discussion and exploration that leads to an agreement, some common ground, between two or more parties holding different views. It may involve bargaining.

It's often seen as belonging in the realm of the statesman, politician or sharp-suited business man or woman, but it is one of the most basic life skills. We negotiate all the time to achieve successful outcomes, with a partner who'd rather go down to the pub than to the cinema, with children over their choice of clothes or bedtime, or with our employers about what we can reasonably do in a working day.

Indeed, if we couldn't create agreement in at least some of these areas, the daily business of living would become, if not intolerable, at least very trying!

Like the assertive person, the successful negotiator is commonly perceived as the one who gets his or her own way; he or she is the winner each and every time. And what's more, he or she is the winner at the expense of the other side. You know this perception is wrong although it does seem to have gained a good deal of ground.

The reason this rather macho view of negotiation has taken hold probably owes more than a little to our history of troubled industrial relations and the rather entrenched and public negotiations between managers and workers. Only a few years ago our TV screens were filled with pictures of ample men in suits from large public organisations and major unions involved in midnight rounds of last-ditch negotiations. Things have changed recently as disputes have declined and co-operation is taking a stronger hold on industrial relations, but in any event negotiation actually does not need to be like this.

All too often, such is the emphasis on winning that negotiators are sometimes prepared to allow a stalemate to happen and not reach an agreement, rather than appear as a loser. The Maastricht Treaty negotiators reached this point with John Major appearing to claim as a victory the fact that at least he hadn't lost the negotiation, even though he might not have entirely won what he wanted for the country. One way of looking at this was that it was a win–lose outcome. And win–lose may be OK for the winner, but it certainly isn't OK for the loser. We'll look at the different outcomes of negotiation a little later in this chapter.

Think of it like this. Suppose you saw a second-hand car for sale in the local paper that was exactly what you wanted, advertised for £1,000. You checked the car and decide you wanted to buy it and offered £900 to the seller, who immediately accepted. Rather than being pleased at securing the car you wanted for the price you wanted to pay, you'd immediately feel cheated. You'd think that you offered too much and that you should have offered less. You might wonder if the fact that the owner took your first offer means that he was desperate to sell and knows something you don't about the car. Perhaps the head gasket is just about to blow.

Then again, you could have offered £850 instead. He might have argued for £950, until you both settled for £900. You would be paying the same amount for the car as in the first example but would feel considerably better about it. So would the seller who, had he accepted your first offer of £900, would be convinced that he sold the car too cheaply. In the second example, both of you are satisfied. And this is what really successful negotiation works towards – everyone coming away with some successes, probably having made some concessions along the way.

The outcomes of negotiation

■ ■ ■

Clearly, there are different outcomes of negotiation – some favourable, some unfavourable.

The following list shows some of the different outcomes and perceptions about negotiations. So you can have:

- lose–lose – clearly unsatisfactory,
- lose–win – OK for one side but not the other,
- win–win – the real result.

This set of options should ring a loud bell, indicating the direct link with assertiveness. Remember, the aim is always a win–win situation.

Lose–lose

Both parties are so eager to make a deal that they accept unacceptable terms.

In the simple one-off purchase, it is very unlikely you'll have a lose–lose situation. It is unlikely that both of you would strike a bad deal. But in more complex negotiations where there is more than one factor to consider in the negotiation, or where a long-term relationship is at stake, both parties can lose out quite easily.

Imagine a protracted and confrontational wages and conditions negotiation. A deal may easily be struck that seems to appease both the board of directors and workers, but if it is inequitable to one side, it could break down within a very short space of time. In that instance, starting again would be so much more difficult for each party, as each would have the bad experience of the first negotiation fresh in their minds.

Or, if a company agrees to wage levels it can't support, the chances are it goes out of business. There may have appeared to be a short-term winner, but in the end everyone loses.

Neville Chamberlain's 'peace in our time' was a classic lose–lose negotiation outcome; fragile, unsatisfactory and ultimately undeliverable. He lost because Hitler didn't comply, and Hitler lost as the war did not end as he had hoped. Unfortunately, they were not the only losers. Millions of others lost out from their posturing and their failure to avert a catastrophic war.

Win–lose

The typical win–lose situation was described earlier when we looked at making an opening offer of £900 for the car that was accepted. Either you'd won, and the seller was desperate to sell but felt he'd let the car go too cheaply afterwards or you'd lost, and felt you'd paid far too much.

This kind of negotiation is very much in the macho school of things – I win; you lose. The long-term impact is on the underlying view of the parties, and their opinion as to whether they have been conned, or out-manoeuvred. The trouble is that in many long-term relationships where people are negotiating for their own interests, the pendulum swings back the other way.

When unemployment is high, a company may squeeze its employees' wage rise, with the threat that other people would work for that money. But if unemployment drops, or a skill shortage appears, the boot's on the other foot. Then the company gets squeezed, as the other side gets its own back.

This is not a healthy long-term relationship for organisations wanting stability and success.

Win–win

Win–win situations are the ideal negotiating outcome. In this case, both parties feel happy with the outcome although it may not be the one they had in mind when they went into the negotiation.

Negotiation, then, is a dynamic process with room for each party to change and adapt their position throughout the negotiation. And this is interesting. If you want to negotiate successfully be prepared for the world to change. Don't go in with a fixed position and accept nothing else – that's an ultimatum, not a negotiating stance.

This is where the first link between negotiation and assertiveness becomes clear. There needs to be give and take, a willingness to listen to the other side, and the ability to put your case, in order to compromise without capitulation. Only if that happens is a win–win situation likely.

Definition

NEGOTIATION

So what is negotiation really about? Negotiation means:

- bringing about agreement between parties with opposing views or different interests – this is why negotiation is at the heart of any successful bid for assertiveness.
- understanding the emotional context in which negotiation take place, with the need for both parties to be winners – this is about respecting people and taking the time to understand them.
- understanding that it is a dynamic process, where the nature of the agreement may shift and tack away from where you originally thought it might be.

You'll recognise that there hasn't been one mention of 'splitting the difference'. Real negotiation is not just about finding the middle point between two arguments and halving the difference. It could mean that one party has to move a long way, while the other shifts only very marginally. All that matters is that the outcome is one they can both live with, and takes account of their different interests.

Part of behaving like a grown-up is to realise that other people can win when we do, and that as the world changes we need to work with those changes and not take entrenched views.

The process of negotiation

Negotiation is a structured activity, with commonly understood moves and countermoves. It is something you need to practise. Watching two good negotiators is like watching two dancers, circling around and responding to each other's movements. They don't lose their cool, they do keep their eye on the outcome.

Only sometimes, when it goes wrong, it's like one dancer trying to do the fox-trot and the other the rumba! Not a good idea because feet get trodden on. Talking of which, look at the following example which shows a situation akin to a good 1977 pogo session.

Case study 5.3

THE HOUSING ASSOCIATION MANAGER

A housing association development manager met up to discuss a new housing scheme with a sales director of a very large house building company. Neither had come to the negotiating table voluntarily; they had been brought together by a mutual partner with whom they both wished to continue working, the local council.

The development manager opened the negotiation by stating that he wanted to upgrade the house builder's 'standard product'. The sales director replied that he wasn't prepared to change anything in the house design or construction.

It looked very much like a log-jam.

Perplexed, the development manager said that he would pay for the changes, if the sales director told him how much extra it would cost. The sales director pointed to the brochure and told the development manager to take it or leave it as it was and stop wasting his time.

The development manager, needing to conclude a deal there and then, decided that there was no room for agreement and refused to conclude the deal.

No deal, no progress.

Who won this negotiation? Clearly, neither party won: both may have damaged their relationship with the local council by failing to agree a deal set up by the council, the sales director has alienated a future client with a great deal of money to spend and the development manager has failed to reach his target by signing a contract to start another batch of new houses. It was a classic case of lose–lose, but why and what could they have done?

The negotiation failed because both parties didn't follow the rules about the process of negotiation. By leaping in part way through the process, they missed out the crucial introductory elements that make a negotiation work. In fact, it would be hard to get it more wrong.

Five steps in negotiation

Go through these five steps and you have a chance of success. Ignore them or skip them and you're asking for trouble.

The five steps are:

1 *preparation* – always important, but particularly so with negotiations;

2 *invitation* – willing partners are more liable to negotiate than unwilling ones, and the invitation sets the all important tone for the negotiations that follow;

3 *presentation* – this is where you put your opening position, where you are starting from;

4 *bargaining* – the cut and thrust, offer and counter offer;

5 *closing the deal* – the agreement and the time to move on.

Let's work through the steps one at a time. As you do, think how they would be helpful in a negotiation situation with one of your team or your manager or a colleague.

Preparation

■ ■ ■

It sounds deceptively simple to say that the outcome of your negotiation depends largely on how well you prepare, but it's true nevertheless.

The first step to set realistic objectives for your negotiation. Aim too high and you'll be disappointed or get into a conflict. Set the aim too low and you'll feel that you have let yourself down. So ask yourself:

- What can I realistically expect to achieve from these negotiations?
- What would I accept and when by?

Three key points have to be covered here – objectives, the other side's strategy and a review of information.

Reviewing information

There is no substitute for going into negotiations with all your information clear. If you don't, the other side may well throw you a question or comment that you can't answer. Collect all the data you think may be relevant, structure it and get it clear. It helps you work out your objective and to see the situation for the opposition's side.

Setting negotiating objectives

Before you ever start talking, work out three levels of outcome:

- your ideal outcome,
- the acceptable outcome,
- a fallback position.

The ideal outcome is naturally what you would most like to achieve. Maybe you want a supplier to give you bigger discounts for smaller quantities, with an improved schedule for deliveries. Hard negotiating may get you there, but it is not a likely outcome.

A more realistic outcome would be where they keep the same level of discount, but you can call off smaller quantities and get fast delivery. Your fallback position is the worst case you are prepared to live with. It's the bare minimum acceptable.

What's their position?

Put yourself in the shoes of the other side and honestly assess the strength of their situation, what they are likely to ask for, and what their three objectives may be. You may not be dead on target, but it will give you a head start.

Envisioning the future

So a key thing before you even start negotiating is to envision the future. Work out where you want to be and how you know you've got there. And in this lies an important theme throughout this whole book. It is crucial that today's manager moves beyond behaving on instinct and impact. She or he needs to be self-reflexive – thinking through and planning what they want to happen and reflecting and learning from what went wrong last time.

So spend a minute to envision the future.

More preparation

Let's take an example. How do you do your preparation before going into a negotiation with a line manager?

Key technique

PRE-NEGOTIATION PREPARATION

Step 1

Well, for a start, before going into a negotiation, you should clear with your manager the limit of your authority. What are you free to negotiate and what is off-limits? We can see this as the negotiation trip-wire. Go over the limit and you trip up.

Find out what your 'tripwire' should be.

Step 2

You should now think about what the other person's moves might be. This is again about envisioning and being prepared for what might happen.

One way to do this is with a simple role play. Practice beforehand with a colleague to work out what you would say if he or she said this or that. To really create the pressure of a real-life negotiating situation, try it out with three or so colleagues. They should fire quick questions at you, one after the other, to test your negotiating skill in a simulation of the negotiation to come. Together, they are likely to come up with all the possible negotiation stances your opponent could take, so you will have a degree of confidence when you face the real thing.

Self-test 5.1

REACTING UNDER FIRE

Try yourself out against some real killer responses to see how you do. Get the people helping you to try lines like:

- *'No way'.*
- *'Get out of my office and don't darken my door again.'*
- *'That's interesting, but I can't do anything about what you suggest for at least six months?'*
- *'Why don't you talk to Peter in finance about this?'*
- *'I thought we'd already sorted that one out.'*
- *'Are you still worried about that?'*
- *'So, you can't cut the mustard.'*
- *'Yes, fine ... at least in principle.'*

Having gone through this mental process, you would be able to go into the negotiation with a strategy: you would know where your tripwires were, what you wanted to say, what the other person was likely to say and when to stay or go.

Invitation

■ ■ ■

The invitation is where you make your first impression. The opening moments can set the tone for a whole negotiation. In the example earlier, the sales director and development manager skipped this stage by being forced together by an important third party, and their negotiation suffered as a result.

At this stage, there are a number of elements of a negotiation that are paramount. They include:

- Your body language. We looked at this earlier, but it really is crucial in negotiations. If you look aggressive or passive then it is unlikely the negotiations will work out successfully.
- How comfortable you and your opponent are. If you feel uncomfortable and awkward, then the negotiations are also likely to be uncomfortable and awkward.
- Some simple things: make the person feel welcome, say 'Hello', offer them a cup of tea, be interested in them.
- Open the discussion up on neutral and friendly ground.
- Make it clear you actually want the negotiation to work.
- Show respect for the other person(s) and the negotiation process; don't undermine the process by being cynical or flippant about it.
- If you have reached agreement with the person before, refer to it to show that it is possible to make a negotiation work.
- Make sure you are both comfortable.
- Don't be coy or evasive.

- The setting and layout of the room is important – it may sound odd, but some room set-ups are almost designed to make negotiations break down. Try some of these horrors.

Checklist 5.1

ROOM TO FAIL - AVOIDABLE PITFALLS

The following set ups are not recommended.

- a big draughty and cold room,
- a noisy room making it hard to communicate,
- big chair, little chair. The person in the little chair feels inferior from the start,
- barriers, like a desk; if one person is sitting behind a desk and the other is placed on the other side it gives the person behind the desk a power advantage. Many negotiators take the desks out of the room completely and simply sit in comfortable chairs to equal out the power.

It's not uncommon for talks to be referred to as 'round table talks'. That's because a round table, or a set of comfortable chairs arranged so everyone appears equal, is a recognised approach to securing a constructive environment. But then there's more than the chairs and table.

Case study 5.4

SALESMEN TELL ALL

At a sales convention, salesmen were asked to reveal their techniques for inviting a negotiation. All maintained eye contact with their opponents and insisted on giving a firm handshake. There, the similarity ended.

- Some deliberately turned up the central heating so that the negotiating arena was uncomfortably warm;
- Some deliberately turned the heating off;

▶

- Some travelled to their opponents' offices and then wrong-footed them by sitting at the head of the boardroom table in a prominent, instead of a subservient, position;
- Some prolonged the meeting until late in the evening without providing refreshments;
- Some tried to sit their opponents in the uncomfortable chairs, with the sun in their eyes.

You will have noticed that all of the above are power moves to show your opponent that you are in a strong position. You also have to show that you are committed to a win–win outcome by showing your interest in them as people.

And the final result?

To show that the conversation WILL be reasonable and adult and that you WILL negotiate an outcome that both of you are happy about.

Presentation

The presentation stage is where you set out your opening position. Based on the assumption that if you ask your opponent for the stars, she might just agree to give you the roof-tops, you should always aim high, while still having the acceptable and fallback positions in mind.

This is not just a silly ritual in negotiating as your opening gambit will have a profound effect on the rest of the negotiation.

Case study 5.5

PITCHING THE OPENING GAMBIT

An engineering union in the 1970s, having considered the views of its members, decided to put in a pay claim for 12 per cent. By accident, the figures were transposed and went to management as a claim for 21 per cent. In the first meeting, management disputed the validity of the 21 per cent pay increase and offered 15 per cent instead. They settled on 18 per cent.

What this shows is the importance of the opening offer in conditioning the response of your opponent. However, a word of warning: if you do not use the value of a shock offer with caution, and sparingly, it will quickly lose its effect for you.

Give and take

This is a factor most of us associate with negotiation, the cut and thrust of offer and counter offer, but it is important to remember that it is only a stage: the development manager and sales director failed to negotiate and reach a satisfactory conclusion because they tried to start at this point, without working through the others.

Negotiation is a highly personal activity, because from the information your opponent takes in, only 8 per cent comes from what you actually say. He/she will pick up 55 per cent of the information you give out from visual stimulus and 37 per cent from your tone of voice. It's vital that you're dressed in the appropriate way, in clothes that you feel comfortable in. Don't try to squeeze into the suit you wore when you were 21, if it means cutting off the circulation to your left leg. If you are uncomfortable, it will show in your posture and your opponent may interpret it as a sign of weakness. Your tone of voice must be firm and professional. There will be plenty of time afterwards for small talk and pleasantries.

Although it is your personal activity which is on display and part of what your opponent is buying into, you must not take what your opponent says personally. Many negotiators are deliberately rude or aggressive to try to unbalance their opponents.

Like the boxer, you must learn to roll with the punches a little so that you can deliver the knock-out blow yourself.

The points to bear in mind are listed below. As you look at them, reflect again on the key parallels between negotiation and assertiveness here – the need to listen to them, say what you think and look for ways forward. The list is:

- Quantify your concessions; if you are going to concede ground plan out carefully what and how much.
- If the other person gives ground, acknowledge it.
- Stay very positive and up-beat.
- Make sure you take time to listen to the other person's stance and respond to it. And when you've listened once, listen again and again and again.
- Control your feelings – don't take things personally, don't show emotion; if you feel anger push it to the back of your mind.
- If you aren't sure what the other person meant, ask a question and find out.
- Don't offer everything early, keep your powder dry.
- Think of yourself as the controller of the orchestra, bringing in new elements and ideas when they are needed.
- Don't be overcome by the hurdles, keep looking for ways around them.
- Always keep your mind open, don't drift off because you might miss something important.

Broadly, there are two negotiation stances your opponent will take. He or she will either take a fixed position or will operate as a principled negotiator. If you learn how to identify each stance, it will help you to position yourself in the negotiation.

The fixed-position negotiator

The negotiator who sticks to one position is not generally an assertive individual ... but often gets away with it from a position of strength. It is a style that is best suited to one-off negotiations, such as where you want to make one purchase or sale to someone you will never deal with again. That's because the effect of this approach can set up a reaction that rebounds later when the other side wants to get its own back.

This style of negotiation is often loud, brash, unreasonable, aggressive and sometimes very effective. The negotiator takes a position and sticks to it – his or her favourite line is take it or leave it. It's almost an ultimatum.

Case study 5.6

SELLING THE FAMILY SILVER

A woman walked into an antique dealer's with a bundle of silver cutlery left to her in an aunt's will. She showed it to the dealer and asked what he would offer.

The offer was £450 but the seller said that she wanted at least £525. The dealer said that wasn't possible – at which point the woman wrapped up her cutlery and walked towards the door. As she opened it, the dealer called her back and offered £500. But she stuck to £525... and the dealer agreed, rather grumpily.

In many negotiating situations there are several issues to be sorted out – price, delivery, size of order and so on. They all have to be tackled as part of the overall package. Positional negotiating works best when there is only one variable to negotiate and usually this is price, although it may be something else like completion or delivery date. That's what the woman with the cutlery did. One price – take it or leave it – and she demonstrated her determination by physically starting to remove from the dealer the option to buy.

Case study 5.7

POSITIONAL BARGAINING IN A BUYER'S OR SELLER'S MARKET

Suppose you went to the International Boat Show with the intention of buying yourself a boat. The first boat you see is a twenty-foot power boat with an enclosed steering point for the skipper. Primarily, it's a day-trip or fishing boat, although there ▶

is a two-berth bunk in the hull. Its asking price is £20,000 and you offer £15,000. The boat owner refuses to accept your offer. You confirm that £15,000 is your best and final offer and, when he still declines to sell it to you, you walk away.

The next boat you like the look of is a hundred-foot motor cruiser. It has two separate decks, sleeps 12 and has a full range of facilities. It even comes with its own jet skis. It will set you back a cool £1.5 million, but it's really what you want. You offer the owner £1.2 million and after some wriggling to try to increase your offer, the boat owner finally accepts.

Positional bargaining worked in the second negotiation but not the first and to understand how to use it, you need to know why. In both cases, you have to put yourself in the other person's shoes. The market for twenty-foot power boats at a moderate price is considerably larger than the market for luxury motor cruisers. The first boat owner knew that he would receive many more sensible offers during the course of the show. The second boat owner knew she was only likely to get one or two serious offers on her boat and was quick to accept a reasonable offer. In other words, if you are the buyer, then positional bargaining will work for you in a buyer's market but fail you miserably in a seller's market.

Also, consider the option that really all you wanted and could afford was the twenty-foot power boat. It could, in fact, have been the boat of your dreams. Once you have taken a positional bargaining stance, it is very difficult to back down and reopen negotiations. You may end up watching someone buy your dream boat for £17,500, which was well within your budget, and watch them sail away into the sunset whilst you are literally left high and dry. Positional bargaining can be a very blunt instrument indeed.

The principled negotiator

The principled negotiator is firm, assertive, calm and collected. He/she would not get flustered by an opponent indulging in a little table-thumping or other bullying tactics. He/she has an agenda to follow, worked out carefully in the preparation stages and will not be rushed into making a mistake.

So what makes up this god or goddess of the negotiating world? The principled negotiator is primarily interested in principles, not positions, and does not allow him/herself to be drawn into detailed or personal exchanges at any stage. The positional negotiator has a number of golden rules that he or she follows:

1 Listen and reflect; don't comment or judge what your opponent says to you.

Case study 5.8

THE APPRAISAL INTERVIEW

In an appraisal interview, a supervisor of a car-hire company told his manager that he would not accept anything less than a 10 per cent performance bonus, or she could find someone else as he'd leave immediately. The company had previously issued guidance to the union that the maximum bonus anyone would receive was 5 per cent and this has been agreed by the union.

In this situation, the supervisor is placing his take-it-or-leave-it offer on the table. The manager has two options in her response. She could also be a positional bargainer and call his bluff with a 5 per cent take-it-or-leave-it-offer. It might work, but undoubtedly, it would sour relations between them. The supervisor would feel humiliated after having to back down and his performance may suffer. Her second option is to take a principled negotiation stance. This is how she might reply.

'I can see that you feel quite strongly about this. Just to clarify, you're looking for a 10 per cent bonus.'

She has acknowledged his feelings, without reacting to the challenge he put down and reflected back to him his request to prove that she is listening. In doing so, she is averting a potential flash point and beginning the process of disarming him.

2 Try to establish the principles behind the position.

The supervisor is putting forward a provocative position in asking for twice the amount his union agreed was reasonable. The manager needs to know whether this is posturing or whether the supervisor does have good reason for this. She continues:

'I'm interested in your thinking. The union has agreed a 5 per cent maximum with its members and you're asking me for twice that. Could you explain a bit more about what brought you to that figure?'

She has shifted him away from a pointless discussion about figures to the principles behind the figures. He may have run a team with twice the productivity of any other team in the company, he may have a particularly demanding and difficult patch to work that he thinks ought to be recognised, or it may be that his team works all the anti-social hours.

3 Try to find common ground and mutual interests.

It's rare in a negotiation for there to be no common ground at all between the parties. If there genuinely is none, then the negotiators have not properly prepared the ground, and have invited each other to negotiate too early. By switching the opponent onto common ground and finding mutual interests, it's possible to draw him/her onto your territory. This is the manager's next step.

'You know, we're not a million miles apart in what we want out of this. We both believe in giving the best service we can to our customers, and that means making sure that the cars are clean and ready when the customer needs them, as well as making sure that there are enough people on the counter to serve them.

'We both recognise that working at 100 miles per hour all the time can be stressful and demoralising and can give you particular challenges as a supervisor to keep staff going. I'd like to say that I think you've done extremely well in trying circumstances over the last six months and I really appreciate your professionalism and dedication. I don't want you to leave and you've put so much into your work that I don't really believe you want to either.'

The supervisor now is beginning to feel valued and understood. The ground is prepared to move the negotiation on.

4 Concessions normally merit a trade-off in return.

There is always the temptation, particularly in a difficult negotiation, to want to appear magnanimous to break a stalemate by making a concession. It may be something that is trivial to you that you don't mind giving up, but it will give the wrong signal to your opponent. In Eskimo folklore, this is encapsulated in the story about the white trader, travelling for the first time from one trading post to another.

He set out with a sled full of meat, groceries and furs and, one day into the wilderness, noticed that he was being shadowed by a wolf. Deciding that the wolf was hungry and attracted by the smell of food, he hacked off a large piece of meat and threw it to the wolf to stop it from attacking. Next day, two wolves appeared and half a side of beef was thrown overboard to appease them. The next day, there were three wolves, the day after that four and by the time he reached the trading post he was accompanied by a whole pack and had nothing but tins and furs left.

Safe in the camp, the trader frantically told his Eskimo hosts how he had only just escaped with his life, only to be told that wolves are curious creatures, quite likely to befriend and accompany someone kind enough to feed them everyday!

The manager needs to trade concessions to move the supervisor over onto her territory.

> *'I can't sanction 10 per cent because 5 per cent is the agreed and set figure. It's outside my scope to throw out national agreements. However, I think we can help in another way. What you're saying to me is that your job is impossible, and much more difficult than the other supervisor's jobs. Your staff have to do the front-of-house bookings, collect the cars and clean them after they come back from customers, whereas your counterparts elsewhere in the company just take bookings. I recognise this point.*
>
> *'Because of the special circumstances, I can release a driver to you, who can take the cars through a carwash, but that will leave*

one of the other depots short. I would need you to handle some of their telephone enquiries and bookings and we could divert one line to you.'

This is setting up a win–win situation for both parties. The supervisor will get the help and support he badly needs and the manager achieves the same, if not a better, service level by imaginative use of resources. By examining the principles, the manager has found out that the supervisor's problem was not really with money but with his working conditions.

Closing the deal

This is the final stage of the negotiation and it needs to be taken as seriously as the others. If you snatch as it too quickly, you may antagonise the other side and reopen the bargaining. If you miss a clear signal that they are ready to agree, they may think that you are not committed to the deal and start to backtrack to save face. Make sure that you watch out for non-verbal signals they may give so that you see the opening when it arrives. A useful way of closing the deal is to recall back what has been agreed, and agreeing any action points that may fall out of it.

Sheila Cane in *Ready Made Activities for Negotiating Skills* says just how important it is to give out signals that you are about to conclude the deal. These include:

- Making relaxed eye contact,
- Smiling at the person,
- Having a relaxed body,
- Putting your hands in a relaxed position.

It is also important at this stage to check how the other person is feeling. Ask yourself whether they really do feel they have won, or whether they are bottling up hurt and resentment. You can also check that any objections have been answered.

Will principled negotiation always work?

■ ■ ■

No. Sometimes you can follow all the steps and find that your opponent does not play by the rules at all. He/she may have a hidden agenda in the negotiation that you are not privy to and may have nothing to do with you or your negotiating ability at all. Perhaps he/she won't negotiate to buy your company's services because your company's car park occupies the area where his/her father had his allotment, and he couldn't stop the planning application. If you think that this is the case, then try a few direct questions like 'is there something else that is bothering you that you haven't mentioned yet?' If all else fails, stop the negotiation and arrange to meet on another day rather than press on to reach a bad agreement.

Resolving conflict using negotiation

■ ■ ■

As a manager, your negotiation skills will be called into play to resolve conflict between colleagues more often than you might like. Your role will be that of a mediator or facilitator, rather than one of the negotiating parties, but the basic rules are the same. So sometimes your role will be to use negotiation to help resolve conflict between team members.

You will be seeking to enable the two parties to reach agreement and must be seen as someone who is:

- committed to resolving the conflict,
- impartial and able to listen fairly to both sides,
- respected by both sides,
- trusted by both sides, particularly in relation to confidentiality.

You may wish to see both sides separately and explain to each first how you will approach it. Depending on the nature of the conflict, you may find it easier to see both parties together for an immediate resolution.

One final look at the assertiveness links

Throughout this chapter on negotiation, the information and examples have followed a very similar pattern to the ABC approach to assertiveness we looked at earlier – especially in situations you know you are going to have to handle.

Remember, in Chapter 3 we looked at some differences between unexpected situations and those you can prepare for – things like having to tell someone they're being made redundant, discussing poor timekeeping or performance with a member of staff, or telling someone that what you promised to do has turned out to be impossible.

These are very similar to negotiating situations even though there are fundamental differences. You may have to adopt a fixed position – you can't change the fact of someone selected for compulsory early retirement in a shake-out of staffing levels, for example. You are essentially just breaking what is probably bad news to them. But you may be able to soften the blow by changing the way they leave, perhaps arranging a phased departure. moving to part-time work with hours that steadily reduce over time.

So while the basic situation is not up for grabs, the details can be negotiated. Moving to a part-time approach could mean that for the organisation, the employee's expertise isn't lost all at once. For the employee, they retain some self-respect as they feel the organisation values their experience, and it gives them the chance to adapt to a new lifestyle more gradually. In other words, assertive behaviour in handling the situation supports the steps in the negotiation process of:

- preparation,
- invitation,
- presentation,
- bargaining,
- closing the deal.

That's it, in the next chapter we look at tips and hints on how to maintain self-control, an important contribution to assertiveness.

Window 5

THE PERFECT NEGOTIATOR

'It was only when I started to learn about assertiveness that I realised that back in my dim and distant past I really had worked with the world's best negotiator.

'I was boss of one department and the person I am talking about was a boss of another department. Frequently, the work fell mid-way between the departments and I would head off down the corridor to discuss with my friend and colleague whose job it was to pick up the work.

'We'd talk and I would put a strong case for the work really being in his camp. He's listen and then say something like: "Yes, that's is interesting, I hear where you are coming from, but it feels to me as though this really is much more your bag than mine".

'He was like the proverbial broken record. Each time, I'd come out of the office quite happy to take on the work.

'He negotiated so skillfully that it didn't actually feel like negotiation. He used the classic assertiveness technique of the broken record – repeating back to me the main points again and again. I use the technique all the time myself now that I know what it is.'

6

Staying in control

Maintaining assertive behaviour means retaining control. That doesn't mean controlling the other person because that's manipulative. Manipulation is a fairly common form of aggressive behaviour that aims to reach a result where the manipulator wins over the others, so it's at the expense of other people and fails to take account of the essential respect for their rights.

It means controlling the process and controlling yourself. In many respects these overlap each other in situations you are dealing with. There are some further techniques that allow you to stay calm, support the basic ABC approach and reinforce it under pressure. In the first part of this chapter we'll cover those.

Then we'll explore how the techniques we've covered help managers raise the standard of their performance, as they work to get the best results from other people's efforts. This is a fundamental aspect of what management is about and it depends largely on giving appropriate and constructive feedback to others on their performance. Feedback helps them know how they're doing, where improvement is needed and where to plan to do better next time. It is not only one of the core tools of management, it is also probably one of the least well used items in the management tool-kit. It tends to come out as either too soft, patronising and passive, or downright rude, aggressive and insulting. By the end you'll see how to use assertiveness techniques to turn feedback into a consistently constructive activity.

Controlling the process

■ ■ ■

Assertiveness is often most helpful in situations that are fraught, difficult and hard to handle. The other person is generally angry or upset and that leads to emotional reactions rather than logical actions. You could be dealing with someone who has a complaint, someone who feels deeply hurt or aggrieved, or an individual who is so hyped-up that they seem completely unable to listen. This sort of emotion can be catching.

How many times have you started out trying to explain something calmly and sensibly, only to find that your temper rises, triggered by the behaviour of the person you're dealing with? For most people this is a real difficulty. When someone else starts shouting, the temptation is to shout back … a bit louder. But it doesn't work. It ends up like two stags locking horns, neither caring about the effect he has on the other and each party determined to win the shouting match. It's the fight side of flight or fight and it leads to a losing situation.

Someone else's failure to listen means that the common sense of the ABC approach stands little chance. You try to show you've listened and you're about to explain how you feel. But they're still in full flow, accusing you of poor service, proclaiming loudly that they have suffered badly, or simply arguing the toss with gusto. What good is the ABC approach now?

The crucial point is that you have to deal with real people and real situations as they are. Examples in books are fine, but they can be written with a happy ending, to prove a point, and life isn't always that simple. We said from the start that there are no magic formulae, so don't feel bad just because extra difficulties have appeared in your path. Stop and think about what these difficulties are; then you can find ways round them.

Your difficulty

Your personal difficulty could be stopping yourself from being drawn into a fruitless, stressful and damaging slanging match.

It is a fairly natural reaction to want to give as good as you get … but if what you're getting isn't much use, it isn't very sensible to want to give the same useless behaviour in return.

There are some techniques you can use to help ensure your inputs are helpful and appropriate. The maxim to work to is this:

Don't react … respond.

The difference is that reaction is generally unplanned and emotional, leading to a loss of self-control. A response, though, can be reasoned and calm, planned and appropriate.

Think it through in advance

When you have advance warning that you are going to have to deal with a difficult situation, you have time to prepare. Think it through from the other person's point of view. Take into account:

- what sort of character they are anyway – if they're normally aggressive, expect fireworks, if they're quiet and submissive, anticipate silence, holding back – maybe even tears;
- how you would feel in their situation – whether you would be angry, upset, hurt or frustrated if you were going to sit where they will be; you can't expect others to feel any less strongly than you would.

Putting off thinking about what will happen does not change the actual event. If the other person is going to become extremely aggressive, they will do so whether you anticipate it or not. So thinking it through in advance does not make the situation any worse. What it does do is help you prepare.

The simple fact that their reaction will not take you by surprise helps you stay in control. You can say to yourself that this is going as you expected – and being able to see the situation objectively means you're less likely to get caught up in a spiral of emotion, and react.

Take three

Even in the best planned situations, someone touching a raw nerve can get you going with an emotional reaction. They may:

- repeat the same point over and over again, although you have explained the situation till you're blue in the face; they aren't listening, so you get frustrated and shout at them; they're missing the point;
- unfairly accuse you of something, as they take out their anger and frustration on the nearest target, which happens to be you;
- say it's all right for you, making you feel they're completely ungrateful and don't know the half of how much you have tried to help them;
- hit the target and say something that is embarrassing – like you (or the people you happen to be representing at the moment) got something wrong, or have failed to keep a promise.

If this happens, count to three and say nothing. It really does help to stop just for an instant, to hold back on your immediate feelings of hurt or indignation. It gives you a much better chance of responding rather than reacting and although it requires a degree of maturity to let pass some comment that you feel you ought to defend, the chances are it was a comment made in anger, without a great deal of justification. In other words, there are many comments made in the heat of the moment that don't merit a reaction.

In any event, you must retain your self-control, and counting to three helps you do that. If you both lose it, the process is out of control and then you've got a real mess on your hands.

Avoid frustration

The need for self-control is particularly important when dealing with aggressive people. But don't forget that passive people can be just as frustrating. Imagine you're in a situation where you are telling someone that because of reduced orders, they are going to have to work fewer hours even though they don't want to. But all they do is keep saying that they see your point of view, and look really sorry for themselves.

It's not unusual for this to be very frustrating, as you want them to open up and say what they really feel. It might be hard to handle, but it would make you feel better if they let themselves go a bit. After a few minutes of passive behaviour it is easy to become so exasperated that you lose control, telling them curtly that you know they don't mean all this, they must feel differently from what they're saying ... and why on earth don't they come out with it and tell the truth!

If you have thought through what will happen, this sort of frustration should be manageable. You're expecting a passive response, so you have had the chance to plan some questions and leading comments that will help them open up. Losing your rag will only make them even more passive and, while it may not appear to matter, the outcome will be that you leave the discussion feeling really bad about yourself and what you have done. It's a positive use of assertiveness skills to get a passive individual to be more open and honest, so you can work on reality.

Their difficulty

The passive person has all the difficulties we touched on in the paragraph above. But it's the aggressive reaction that gives us the most difficulty. Handling an angry reaction that turns into an attack requires real control.

Their problem is that if they are so wound up that they can't find time or space to listen, they will never be party to the win–win situation you're pursuing. You have a responsibility to help them come in from the cold, to overcome their difficulty. Put simply, the most common difficulty is the inability to listen.

Slowing them down

Anyone who is getting major emotional issues off their chest is not in the best frame of mind for listening. They may not even hear the fact that you have taken the first step in the ABC process and said you've heard them.

Sometimes, though, the first step takes the wind right out of their sails – especially if it's an apparently major row that grows out of a simple misunderstanding, one that can be sorted out with little or no effort as long as someone stays cool.

Case study 6.1

I'M HERE TO TELL YOU ...

The works director of a firm was basically a nice guy, but things had been stressful lately. To cap it all, the new sales manager kept parking in his space. For a time he said nothing, but the feeling of resentment grew until he was really angry and out of control.

He stormed into the new manager's office and let rip. 'I don't know who the hell you think you are, but I've had enough of this. Every damn day you park in my space by the main entrance. I've given you the chance to stop but have you? No, it's becoming a fixture.'

The new manager broke in and said, 'Yes, I can see my parking there is wrong'. It wrong-footed the director.

Saying 'Yes' was basically all it took. The director carried on with the tirade for a couple of seconds, but as the 'yes' sank in he stopped and said, 'Oh ... right'. His slowing down gave the manager the chance to explain. 'I'm sorry you're upset, and it won't happen again. However, nobody told me where to park and where not to, so it was a genuine misunderstanding. Do you want me to go and move now?'

The director lost virtually all the anger, and became almost apologetic. 'Sorry I blew up ... it's a bit tricky at the moment. Somebody should have told you – maybe I should have. Anyway, no hard feelings.'

You'll notice that the manager did not apologise for something that she felt was not her fault, but did accept the situation. By agreeing that the director had a factual point she removed the heat from the confrontation and brought things down to a workable level. She managed to avoid a trivial irritation turning into a major issue, an occurrence that is all too common. In effect, she made the director lose his bearings for a moment.

This is a useful technique.

Clouding the issue

The car parking example contains the bones of a technique that helps you slow aggressive people down so they do hear what is being said. It works by removing from them their feeling of being in control, the sense that they know exactly where they are and what they're saying.

Think of taking a motorboat across a stretch of open water. Wonderful visibility, the sun in the sky and not another boat in sight. The route to the other side of the bay is clear, and the person at the helm can relax. Aim the boat in the right direction, get it going and keep it going. If the wind is against them it just means making a bit of extra effort to keep moving forward, but they know where they're heading and they can defeat the headwind with a bit more engine power.

That's what it's like for someone who continues to bluster and shout when they're aggressive. They know where they are, they are clear on what they want to say and there's nothing to stop them. Once they're moving they're not going to slow down for someone who argues with them – in fact they will work even harder to get the point across.

But what if a heavy cloud bank descends around the boat, blotting out all the landmarks and adding to the risk that there could be another vessel lurking out there somewhere? How do the sailors cope then? They slow the engine down, take another look at the chart and the compass, and become infinitely more conscious of where they are and what's happening around them. They then proceed carefully and with more awareness that they're in danger of losing their bearings.

Agreeing with someone who is determined to make a point often has the same effect. Saying, 'Yes, I can see that you're angry about this', goes a long way towards making them realise they've reached their aim. The other person is agreeing, and there's no need to keep arguing. Of course, it isn't always that quick and simple and it may need a few attempts, but before long it has the effect of slowing them down.

But what have you agreed to? Surely you've lost all control if you agree they're right? The vital point is that you haven't conceded anything. What you say recognises the way they feel, or the fact that they're upset or frustrated; it doesn't say they're right to feel that way.

This can be a difficult technique to get to grips with, so we'll explain it again.

You agree that you can see why they feel as they do, but you don't agree that their argument is right, at this stage. So the sort of statement to make that clouds the issue and makes them unsure about their bearings is one that says:

- *'Yes, I can see this has made you angry.'*
- *'Clearly you're upset by this.'*
- *'You feel really let down, obviously.'*
- *'I understand that you think I (or the company) got it wrong.'*

See the approach? You're ensuring that they hear you say you have listened to them, but you're saying it in a more powerful way than the basic step outlined in the ABC approach. You haven't said that the company was wrong, just that you can see they think that. It may seem like a fine point, but it is crucial. It preserves your integrity, and allows you to be honest in the way you recognise their views and feelings.

The technique has one purpose and one purpose only: to get them to hear you say that you have listened to their point of view. Unless you achieve this purpose, you cannot proceed to the second stage of saying what you think.

Once you have established communication – and that's what you're doing, given that communication is a two-way process – you can start to explain your viewpoint. However, if they're wound up, they may not listen to you – and that's where you can use another technique for helping them overcome their difficulty.

Play it again ... and again, Sam

What's the most obvious thing to do when someone obviously hasn't heard what you said, and keeps saying something different or raising new issues? That's right ... you say it again.

It sounds too simple to be true, but think about it. In a heated discussion, once you've made one point you move on to the next, on the assumption that they heard what you said. The argument goes off in different directions and if you keep reacting rather than responding, you end up with a verbal game of tennis. Words and comments are knocked back and forth at such a speed that nobody can really remember what the game's all about. What you said hasn't sunk in, and you need to do something about it.

You have established for them that you have heard them, either with the ABC approach or by clouding the issue. Now you need to get your point across and it could take quite a few repetitions of the same message before it sinks in. Here's an example of what we mean.

Case study 6.2

I CAN'T MAKE IT ...

'It's no good telling me you can't get there. The meeting tomorrow is at 4.30, so I want you there at least half an hour before that.'

'I know that's what you would like; however I simply can't do it. I'm meeting the Council people until at least 3.30 and by the time I get back it will be later than that.'

'It's vital that you're here for that 4 o'clock pre-meeting session. We need to sort our plans out before we see the architect. Do what you have to ... but be there.'

'Yes, we do need to have a strategy worked out, and I would love to be there. Unfortunately I can't be in two places at once, so while I can get there by 4.15, I just can't promise 4 o'clock.'

'Look – I'm not happy about this. I'm sure you can do it and I don't know why you're being so obstinate this time. You've always managed it before so I'm counting on you.'

▶

'I know you're not happy; neither am I. I can make 4.15, Gus, but 4 o'clock is cutting it too fine. I'm not being awkward even though I am being obstinate – and that's only because I'm not going to promise something I can't deliver. Why don't you start with the others and I'll catch you up. And if you like I can see you later for ten minutes, to give you my initial thoughts, so you have them in mind while I'm not there. I can't promise 4 o'clock, though.'

'OK, if that's really the best you can do. Come up at two this afternoon and we'll see where we are.'

This simple repetition of the same point, dressed up in different ways, explains the situation consistently while avoiding sounding simply bloody-minded. It has all the characteristics of effective assertiveness and it plays the same message over and over again, until the person it's directed at has to accept it. If the person going to meet the Council had given up under pressure, the result would have been either an ineffective meeting with the Council, or a later arrival in Gus's office than was agreed.

This technique is especially important and particularly powerful. It helps in the common situation when someone else isn't listening, but it does take practice. If you're not in control of yourself and the process, you'll miss the vital signs from the other person's reactions as to whether or not they have heard you.

The main problem with it is that it can seem awkward and false, when you're reading about it here or on the first few occasions you use it. However, it does work and it really makes a difference, so try it out. Like the other techniques we cover, you may feel that they are so transparent that the other people you're dealing with will think you've flipped. Surely they will spot that you're plodding away at a technique that interferes with normal speech patterns? But they don't, they really don't. Obviously, if you said the same thing word for word each time, with the same intonation at the same pace, you'd sound like a Dalek and that would raise the odd eyebrow. But paraphrasing the message and coming at it over and over again from a slightly different angle slips by entirely unnoticed. After all, they're not really listening to you, so they won't hear every syllable anyway.

Where are we now?

■ ■ ■

It's worth spending a few minutes confirming which techniques you have explored so far and how they all fit together. Remember, the foundation for these techniques is the belief and the values, the acknowledgement of rights and responsibilities. Then building on that you have:

- the basic ABC approach where you:
  - listen to them,
  - show you've heard them,
  - say what you want to say,
  - propose a way forward – action that benefits everyone;
- the need to watch body language, so the verbal message is not overpowered by conflicting signals in your face, posture, hands and so on;
- preparation and thinking it through, to anticipate what sort of behaviour you are likely to encounter and be ready for it;
- counting to three when you feel tempted to react, so you stay in control of yourself and the situation;
- slowing them down and clouding the issue so you take the wind out of their sails, by acknowledging how they feel without conceding your position;
- repeating the message if they haven't heard you the first time … until they do and you know they do.

In the next chapter we'll look at some more sophisticated techniques as well, for use when you've got the ones listed here working well and you're comfortable with them. We're not putting them all together, up front, because it is easy to overload someone with techniques and tips. If you were to work on everything at once you would be watching your body language, thinking about what to say next, monitoring how the conversation was going and trying to work out the next move, all at the same time. Then you would find it hard to look natural! Start with the ABC, practise using it until it feels comfortable and forms part of your normal everyday behaviour. Then you can add other approaches. But don't be too ambitious all at once. It can lead to disappointment.

Giving feedback assertively

■ ■ ■

Assertiveness is not only about handling crisis situations that come your way, triggered by someone else. It's not just about complaining people, aggressive bosses and individuals who won't listen. There is an active side to it, where you use assertiveness to enhance your everyday performance, putting assertiveness to work in your routine management communications around the organisation so you get better results.

This issue of results is at the heart of what managers do.

> ***Definition***
>
> ***MANAGEMENT***
>
> Managers exist to achieve success and one definition of management is that it *achieves results through other people*.

This is sometimes a problem for managers who don't like letting go of the last job, and taking on the role of planning, co-ordinating and improving operations. You are very likely to have encountered fairly senior people who seem to want to do the jobs of the people they now manage, preferring to be hands-on rather than strategic. If this sounds like you, then it's a problem you need to address … but that's another book.

The definition that says you get results through other people means you must help individuals and teams plan and deliver their achievements, so they combine with those of colleagues and produce the results you're judged on as a manager. Your job is bigger than those of the people working for you. One group working for you produces one part of the service or product, another of your teams handles a different part of the process and you are accountable for the whole thing. In other words, your success is entirely dependent on their achievement.

Given this fact, it is in any manager's interests to work at helping the people they manage to:

- maintain the quality of what they are already doing well,
- identify where they could do better,
- plan how to make the improvements.

Similarly, unless you believe that human beings at work like getting things wrong and achieving less than they are capable of, then it follows that the people being managed also want to know about the same three things. Look at it from your own perspective and think about whether you appreciate someone giving you feedback on what you do well. Everyone does … and it happens too infrequently in many organisations. A word of praise for a job well done makes such a tremendous difference to morale and relationships, and it costs nothing.

Then go a stage further and ask yourself whether you would accept comments from the person who gave you positive feedback, on where you could do better, why and how. Invariably, the answer is that it depends on how the feedback is phrased and delivered. The most common statement is that, 'I welcome feedback, as long as it's constructive'.

Constructive feedback

The basis of feedback is that the spectator often sees more of the game than the players. A manager or a colleague has the benefit of observing what someone else does and what effect it has on them, the observer. That puts them in a position where they have information that the other person (we'll call them a learner, for now) doesn't have about themselves and their actions. The feedback process works when the observer shares that information in a way that leads to insight on the part of the person observed, that can be channelled into improvement action.

Constructive feedback is based on facts and evidence rather than opinion or qualitative judgements. That's because anyone wanting to change their behaviour needs to know factually what needs attention. It's possible to work out action to make improvements if someone tells you:

'When you spoke to the group I couldn't hear you at the back. You spoke softly and looked down at your notes quite a lot.'

On the other hand, if they say:

'You need to improve your delivery',

there's no indication of exactly what needs doing. Where do you start?

It's not what you say...

Constructive does not mean congratulatory, or positive. It means with care and genuine concern for the other person. Constructive feedback needs to cover both positive and negative points, as the learner can't improve if all they get is praise for the good points. So it is not what is said, it is how it's said.

There are some basic rules for giving constructive feedback.

Checklist 6.1

FEEDBACK

- *Give feedback at the right time* – while it may seem appropriate for a manager to give feedback at any time, there are occasions when it is inappropriate; someone who is not ready or willing to receive comments will not take them on board, so it's important to check that there is adequate time and the recipient is aware of what is to happen. Never leave it too long, though – it becomes more and more difficult to relate the feedback to the events once they have started to fade in memory. This is especially true if it's feedback on poor performance.

- *Start with something positive* – praising someone opens their minds more to negative comments, and leads them to accept them from someone who clearly has a balanced view.
- *Own the feedback* – say 'I felt' or 'I found' and not, 'everyone thinks ...' because it increases the power of the message, makes it more personal and caring and also excludes the possibility that you could make false assumptions about what other people think.
- *Describe rather than evaluate* – if someone does not speak up in a meeting so you can't hear them, say you couldn't hear and avoid comments like, 'Your delivery isn't good enough'. This gives them a clear picture of the effect their actions had on other people.
- *Be specific* – give examples of actual events and explain why they were good or bad in your view; avoid waffling about generalities and focus on issues that both parties can relate to.
- *Focus on things that can be improved* and ignore things that can't be changed – there's no point in telling someone it would be better if they were 20 years younger.
- *Offer options for consideration* but don't preach – for the person you couldn't hear in the meeting, you could say, 'Maybe next time you could think about directing your voice more to the back ... or you could just talk more loudly and slowly ... or there's always a microphone'. You're not telling someone what to do, just offering some ideas about how to tackle what they need to tackle. They are free to ignore your suggestions and find their own solution in other ways.
- *End with a positive comment* so they leave on a high note. It increases the motivation to improve and reinforces the value of the negative comments.

If someone asked you to describe styles of giving feedback that are assertive, passive or aggressive, what would you come up with? The chances are that you would say something like this:

- Assertive feedback respects the other person, shows you have observed and listened to them, explains factually what you feel and makes appropriate suggestions for improvement; in other words, constructive feedback as we have described it here is assertive.
- Feedback given aggressively targets only the poor aspects of performance and puts people down; there's no praise for what was good, no ownership of the issues and no real help in moving forward – just criticism that provides no basis on which to work for improvement, that often appears in appraisal interviews as, 'You ought to do this better, that faster and the other thing properly. I'm warning you to pull your socks up'.
- Passive feedback comes across as all good – no mention of problems or areas for improvement; it's another common approach that managers take in appraisal interviews, when it comes out as, 'It's all fine … everything's hunky-dory so just keep going. You're a great person and I'll leave it to you'.

Case study 6.3

THE HEALTH AND SAFETY TRAINING SESSION

A tyre factory supervisor was running a workplace health and safety training session, on fume and dust control. Part of his personal development was a National Vocational Qualification (NVQ) in delivering training. He had to demonstrate competent performance in running a session to an assessor, to gain a credit towards the qualification.

Before calling in an external assessor, the supervisor's boss (the departmental manager) agreed they'd hold a dry run. The manager compiled a set of criteria for success that covered the key aspects an assessor would look for – things like sound technique in using the flip chart and overhead projector. At the end of the session they held a feedback session. The manager – trained in the use of constructive feedback – gave comments as follows.

'As we agreed, I'd like to give you some feedback on the session. OK? Good. I thought your manner and the way you approached

the subject brought the topic to life – and it's not really a hugely exciting issue for most people. One specially good technique you used was when you asked them a question and let them discuss a range of ideas – like when you asked how they would expect their sons and daughters to be protected if they worked here.

'Your diagrams on the screen were clear enough for me to follow your explanation in detail. However, there were a couple of occasions when I couldn't see the diagrams on the screen from that side of the room. I checked afterwards and I couldn't see from further round, either. The screen was at a difficult angle; one way of sorting that out is to sit in all the seats yourself before the others come in, to check they all have a good view.

'I liked the way you kept notes going on the flip chart. It made me feel reassured that I could always look back and remind myself what we'd covered. Pale green doesn't show up well, though, so maybe you could consider getting some darker colour pens, so they make a real impact.

'The start of the session interested me, and the summing up made sense. I got a bit lost in the middle, when you were looking at the industry definition of fume. Simple language would have made it easier for me to follow.

'Overall, though, I felt that I had been given a detailed view of the issues, and I knew what to do by the end. There's a lot there that is up to NVQ standard already, and with a bit of polishing on the points I've made you should be ready for a full assessment. I think you did really well.'

If you compare the way this feedback was given against the checklist, you'll see it has all the components of constructive and assertive feedback. There are criticisms, but they don't come across as hard to take. You can imagine the supervisor nodding in agreement as the areas for improvement are talked through – the screen angle, the flip chart work and the clarity of content in the middle of the session.

Aggressive feedback would have picked on the areas for improvement only. A passive version would have stressed the positives and, if the faults had been mentioned, they would have been prefaced with something like, 'I may be nit-picking, and it's probably just me, but …'. The crucial fact about aggressive and passive feedbacks is that they are far less likely to be acted on, and to make a real difference to performance. The assertive feedback is direct, honest and helpful, delivered with openness and a clear interest in both the supervisor and his work.

Another positive point about sound feedback is that it is far less common for the recipient to leap to their own defence, and justify what they did wrong. Once someone starts to put forward a justification for their own poor performance, it becomes real in their minds, and they steadily raise the barriers to taking on any suggestions for improvement. However, if the supervisor had tried to excuse the screen angle or the green pens, the manager's line would have been to adopt the ABC approach, probably reinforced by repeating the message until it got through.

So, constructive feedback and assertiveness go hand-in-hand. If you add this to the fact that effective negotiation has such strong similarities with the basics of assertive behaviour, the relevance of the techniques and beliefs we're talking about becomes ever greater. Assertiveness moves in from being a peripheral issue, towards the centre of effective management behaviour in a number of different guises.

The assertiveness window in this section looks at how even the experts sometimes find it hard to apply the techniques of assertiveness.

Window 6

MAKING ASSERTIVENESS WORK

It takes time and practice to learn how to be really assertive. Don't be put off if at first things don't seem to work the way you want.

Trying to be assertive and not knowing how can cause greater problems than it attempts to solve. A typical example is cited by psychologist Eddy Knasel.

'My mother-in-law, Carol, once saw an old lady on a bus being picked on by a group of school children. They were calling the lady names, generally taking the mickey and being very unpleasant. Carol decided to intervene and told them to stop behaving so badly. The kids' behaviour only got worse. They reacted badly to being told what to do by a stranger – and responded to what they saw as her aggression by spitting at her. An assertive approach would have been to ask them why they were behaving in that way – a question they probably wouldn't have been able to answer.'

However, sometimes even professional assertiveness trainers can feel they aren't succeeding. Eddy Knasel experienced this himself.

'Recently, I was involved in a "role play" day to work out how to run a new training programme. In one scenario I had to deal with a stroppy employer, determined not to give me any information about his company.

'I'm an experienced interviewer and assertiveness trainer. I know how to use all the right techniques. As the "manager" got angrier I behaved perfectly, working to defuse his anger, empathise but state my point of view and so on. After five to ten minutes I usually win. Not this time!

'Role play means taking on a character, sticking to their script … being nice and compromising wasn't in the script. The "manager" didn't respond as I planned and at the end of the session I felt I had failed miserably. The feedback I received from the other trainers was excellent but it didn't make me feel any better about my performance. When I came to do an interview with a real life manager – who blocked my questions and I felt had something to hide – after five or ten minutes the techniques worked.'

Not succeeding doesn't mean you're doing anything wrong. Have faith in your abilities and don't give up – most of the time being assertive will pay off.

7

Moving ahead

In this final chapter we'll look at some further techniques you can call on once the basics are well established. Then you'll have the chance to look at some common and difficult situations, so you can see what sort of assertive approach you would use. Finally, there's a look at the need to monitor your progress in developing assertive behaviour, and the chance to make plans that will help take you further forward.

Some further techniques

In Chapter 4 you first came across the ABC approach. Just to remind you of its key points, because you'll need to remember it as you work with the further techniques in this chapter, it operates like this:

Actively listen – and show you're listening.

Be clear about your own views, feelings and beliefs.

Come to an agreed decision about what will work best in the circumstances.

In addition to this basic ABC approach there are some other fairly specific and sophisticated techniques that extend its range and scope, and are helpful in certain situations.

The ones we'll look at here are:

- assertive thinking,
- stating feelings,
- what matters most,
- spelling out the consequences.

Assertive thinking

■ ■ ■

If you play any sport, or take part in any challenging personal activity – like drama, creative writing or painting – you may have come across this already. Look in on a set of bobsleigh drivers in the changing room, as they prepare to hurtle downhill at breakneck speed and you'll see them sitting quietly with their eyes shut. Their heads and bodies turn and lean first one way, then the other, as they run through the course in their minds before they compete. It's as if they are watching a video of the course, or in a virtual reality scenario. In their minds they're on the course, anticipating all the turns and banking and planning how to get through the difficulties most smoothly.

In assertiveness, it's simply the same question of thinking positively about what is to come, so you confirm to yourself that you can cope and you plan where some specific techniques may fit. Like many of the other techniques, it looks pretty obvious, but it is so effective that it merits attention in its own right.

The basic issue is this. If you believe you can't do something … you won't. If you believe you can … you probably will; and even if you don't get it completely right, there is a fair chance of success.

Take a situation where you are going for an interview for a new job. What will happen, do you think, if you go along convinced in your own mind that you won't get it, because you haven't got the experience they probably want, or because there's bound to be a better candidate? You've got it … or rather, you won't get it. It becomes a self-fulfilling prophecy. Any golfer who has looked at a three-foot putt and said to himself that it probably won't go in knows this. It's accepting defeat and failure before you ever get started.

The following example is based on a story told to us by a manager we encountered during research, who asked to remain anonymous.

Case study 7.1

THE BUDGET MEETING

Pat Smith runs the distribution section in a small and specialised book publishers. Each year the section heads come together and agree the budget and year after year Pat's budget has been held back as others put up a better case and take the lion's share.

The year before last, Pat was the only section head who took the opportunity to attend a series of assertiveness seminars, and came away convinced that it could make a difference. Having worked on the basic techniques it became part of everyday behaviour, in one-to-one situations. But the annual budget meeting was looming and Pat was uncertain about the future. The section needed two new shrink-wrapping machines, to cut packing time and save money in the long run. But other section heads had always shouted louder in the past, and ended up getting their own way at Pat's expense.

Pat pondered previous passive performance. Before it had always felt as if there was little point in even trying – the distribution section was bound to lose because they always did. But this year ... maybe it could be different. Pat went through the list of techniques available and ended up thinking, 'I *can* do this; I have as much right as the others and I know ways of getting my point across assertively. I don't mind making concessions if the other sections really have a better case than mine – but I know that my case is really strong. I shall go in there as an equal and use the skills I've got, that they haven't. I know I can get a result.'

The outcome was that Pat didn't get the two machines, because the company was suffering from low orders and a cashflow problem;

but one was agreed and it made a huge difference. The following year, armed with figures on how much this one machine had saved, Pat went to the budget meeting and got the second. In Pat's mind the success is attributable very largely to positive thinking.

Developing a positive mental attitude depends on having evidence that leads you to know you can succeed. If you go into a really difficult negotiation armed only with faith, it may not get you all the way. But in Pat's case there had been two years of working to develop assertiveness, so the positive approach was rooted in evidence from smaller successes.

Stating feelings

The reason this approach has been left until now is that it requires a direct confrontation with someone whose behaviour is affecting you adversely. It takes a bit of bravery and confidence, which comes only after you've mastered the basics. We'll look at a couple of example situations.

Case study 7.2

A CONFLICT SITUATION

You're in a situation where you are discussing a disciplinary issue with an employee – someone who is pretty outspoken and direct. You have reminded yourself that the purpose of the disciplinary procedure is to clarify with someone which of their actions are unacceptable, so that they can be improved and the problem resolved. It isn't a process of setting out to 'get' someone.

This individual been arriving late for work regularly and you have to do something about it because:

- the fact that someone is apparently challenging your authority is starting to undermine your position;
- the tasks this individual does come at the start of the process; other people are prevented from getting on with their work if this person fails to pass things on to them;

- the boss is watching you – vague comments have been made about your need to exercise more authority;
- you're stressed about it; you've tried all sorts of ways of overcoming the problem and have felt guilty consistently as the individual concerned has not responded to your supportive approach.

You arrange to see them and they come in and shut the door. As you begin to explain that you are concerned that their lateness is having an adverse effect on the department, and that this is the first part of the formal disciplinary procedure, they begin to get very argumentative. Their language descends towards the vernacular and their body language begins to take on a more aggressive tone.

However, the main problem is that they accuse you of picking on them and their comments become quite personal. You are offended by this and decide to say something … but what? The temptation is to shout them down and play the heavy manager – after all, authority is on your side. But why should you reduce yourself to their level? It would only make you feel upset and annoyed with yourself for the rest of the day – and make it harder to look them in the eye once this is all over.

Instead, you reach for an assertiveness tool – stating feelings. You say exactly what it is about their behaviour and their approach that gives you offence – head on, but calmly and firmly.

'Look, I know you're wound up and I'm happy to hear what you have to say. However, swearing at me and becoming aggressive does not help to sort this out; in fact it makes things worse. I find it offensive and it gets in the way. I'd like you to take a few deep breaths and start again – without the language this time.'

Maybe it will take some time for the message to sink in … maybe you'll need to repeat it quite a few times, but you have every right to tell the other person what it is in their behaviour that you find unacceptable. It's not enough just to get angry in return, and snap, 'Don't you swear at me, or …!' because that simply ratchets the conflict up a notch or two.

Stating your feelings in this sort of situation meets all the criteria for assertiveness. It is likely to get a result, and at the very least it leaves you feeling much happier, more confident and less stressed than you would if you had joined in the fight.

Case study 7.3

A LONG-STANDING IRRITANT

Another common situation arises when someone does something that you find really annoying, or that has a negative effect on you or your work.

For instance, someone perpetually turns up late at a meeting that you are chairing. You can either:

- pass some sarcastic comment in the hope of hurting them enough so they conform;

- ignore the problem and hope it goes away, and do nothing in case it turns into an argument;
- make the problem worse by waiting for them to arrive each time (at the expense of the people have bothered to turn up on time) and then maybe stopping the meeting to recap on what they've missed;
- handle it assertively, stating your feelings.

In any event, this is aggressive behaviour on their part – they take no account of the rights of others and impose their own requirements on the group.

The only positive way forward is the assertive way, and you can use an approach that is very similar to the ABC approach to handle it. After the meeting you ask for a word and say something like this.

'I appreciate that you're busy. However, you have turned up late to the last six meetings. We are all busy and waiting for you takes up our valuable time, and it makes my job as chair a great deal harder. I don't think you're being fair to me or the others, and I want to establish that you will be there on time in future.'

It is a staged approach, like the ABC, where you:

- say what behaviour offends you;
- explain the effects of it on you;
- explain how it makes you feel;
- state what you want to happen in future.

It could be that the person concerned had no idea that they caused such disruption. If that is the case – and self-centred behaviour like this frequently is founded on lack of thought rather than malice – you will find that approaching the problem directly, firmly and clearly has an immediate and major effect for the better.

If they start to make excuses about pressures of work, being held up by other meetings and so on, it's back to the ABC approach. You might say:

> *'I appreciate that it's hard to get away from the telephone – we all have the same problem. However, this meeting is important to all of us and I would like you to find a way of getting there for a prompt start'.*

The bottom line is that it's not up to you to solve their problem – your aim is to get them to help solve yours. Stating your feelings clearly is a powerful technique for cutting through distracting and ancillary issues, so you get to the heart of the matter. Like other techniques, when you see it spelt out it looks like a simple use of appropriate behaviour, saying things that you are entitled to say.

So is the next technique we'll look at, one for clarifying what you are meant to do when you're being pulled in two directions at once.

What matters most

■ ■ ■

You get mixed and conflicting messages all the time. There are many opportunities for contradictions and discrepancies to turn up and put you in an impossible position. Unless, that is, you tackle them assertively.

Let's look at three common situations and how you could handle them.

What are you saying ...

One fairly regular example crops up when someone is behaving aggressively and comes out with clearly inconsistent messages. Think about having to explain to an employee that their work still is below standard, despite a series of attempts to improve it.

In the meeting they become angry and flustered and they make contradictory points in the same statement that indicate they're losing their way and are out of control.

> *'I've tried really hard to get this right. It's not fair that you keep picking on me; I'm starting to think this is personal. I don't care anyway – I don't think it's an important part of the job.'*

You want to bring them back to a more self-controlled state, so you identify the contradictions and ask them what they really mean.

> *'Now hang on ... I know you've tried really hard but now you say you don't care anyway. Which is it? Is it worth trying hard for or not?'*

It's likely that all the signs are that they do care, and are raising defences to avoid discussing the real issues – which is exactly what you do want to discuss. By highlighting the discrepancy you make them stop and think, and confirm what they really mean. That's important, because you need to know what their reality is, so you work with them on the basis of accurate facts and feelings, to plan the next moves.

It's all urgent!

There are several occasions when you are told that one piece of work is crucial, only to be told later by the same person that something else has suddenly assumed greater importance. Having arranged things so that you can meet the deadline for the first one, you are given a conflicting message about priorities. But the first activity hasn't been crossed off the list. It's still important and the chances are that it remains a priority with an unchanged deadline – all that's happened is that an extra task has been added to the load. The net result is likely to be that neither can be completed successfully if they're competing for your time and resources, so this situation cannot be allowed to slip.

Fortunately, handling this sort of situation is fairly straightforward. It's the ABC approach with a clear focus on the discrepancy. You need the other person to decide what is more important, so you know what you are doing and so that they can make plans to get both jobs covered.

'Earlier, Jan, you said that I had to crack on with this one. Now it seems the goal posts have shifted and that one is top priority. Which is it, please? I can't finish both and if I'm to get it right I need you to clarify what you want me to do.'

This may get the desired result first time … but people being what they are, it's very possible that you'll hear something like this:

'They're both urgent – I need it all done.'

But you can't do it – you know that. So under no circumstances say that you'll do your best. It won't be good enough. You may have to come back with repetition of the message, clouding the issue and even stating your feelings to get them to hear you, but you must stick at it. In the following response we've indicated where various techniques come into play and build on each other.

… having counted to three rather than lose control …

'Yes, I know they're both urgent and I can see you're under pressure from the boss.'

Step A in the ABC, supported by Clouding the Issue

'However, I can't do both in the time.'

Step B, supported by Repeating the Message

'I find it really difficult to plan properly when the priorities change so often …'

Step B again, with Stating Feelings

'... so I need a clear instruction please, on which to do.'

Step C

'It has to be one or the other, because there just isn't time for both.'

Repeating the Message

Seeing all the techniques working together like this should illustrate that they don't have to come across as contrived or false. The response is sensible, factual and assertive. It should achieve results – but if it doesn't you just stick at it and use appropriate techniques again – especially repeating the message.

Remember though, it's not only about you sorting out your problems; assertiveness is about winners all round, so you aim to help them achieve success as well. By telling you to get on with one job, the other person now has no one working on the second one. It may be that you can add something to Step C that can help reach a sensible compromise.

'I could do three quarters of both, if you found out which bits have to be done first, or maybe someone else could pick up one job? Derek is working on that long-term project, so his section may be worth a try.'

Don't listen to them, listen to me ...

Another situation is where one person says clearly that X is the top priority, so you get to work on it. Then another individual comes along and asks curtly why on earth you're working on X, when Y is obviously where your efforts ought to be going. To make matters worse, before you know it they turn on their heel and leave you trying to balance two contradictory instructions about what to do next.

This is especially common in organisations with a form of matrix management – say a service engineer based in a district office, responsible to both the district manager in the local office and the service manager at headquarters. The problem here is different from one boss giving you contradictory instructions. In this case you need to get the two individuals to sort it out between them, or you will stay as piggy in the middle. It really is a potential no-win situation.

The approach is simple. It's still a question of following the ABC line and explaining the situation clearly – but then it always is. All the techniques we suggest start with that common foundation.

It's the outcome that has to be different. Here, you need to get the district manager (your line manager) and the service manager (heading the technical function) to agree a consistent line, and that means making them talk to each other. It is potentially very tricky, as each individual may tell you to listen to them and to take no notice of their counterpart. But you can't do that – you're bound to displease one of them whatever you do.

> *'Look, I'm confused. Frankie was on the phone just now saying I have to do the paperwork first, now you're telling me that's not important. What I'll do is start the other job in the meantime, and maybe you could agree with Frankie what you both want me to do. It's a management decision and if it's a mess it will reflect badly on the district and the service department ... and nobody wants that. If I choose I'm bound to get it 50 per cent wrong, so could you let me know by lunchtime what you and Frankie have agreed, please?'*

There is also a last resort option – spelling out the consequences, the technique we look at next. In this case you could legitimately say that as this is a management decision, it's not one that should rebound on you.

> *'I need to hear from you by half past two, if I'm to get it done on time. You've done this job, so you know I have to have an answer by then. What I could do if you like is check with Hector, the director, on what the procedure is. I was going to do that before I rang you, but I felt a bit foolish so I rang you first. Still, I'm happy to ring him now if you think that's the best approach.'*

It is a heavy option, but sometimes tough problems call for tough solutions.

Spelling out the consequences

As well as the example immediately prior to this, think back to the situation when we explored the need to state your feelings.

Remember, someone was turning up late and you were considering disciplinary action? It was made clear then that disciplinary procedures exist to help remove unsatisfactory behaviour and performance. That doesn't always mean coming down hard on someone and aiming to sack them. If the person at fault can improve their performance through training, coaching – or even a little extra effort – the desired result is achieved.

If we were studying disciplinary procedures in any detail, you would see several key elements in a disciplinary interview, including the need to be specific and unambiguous about:

- what behaviour is unacceptable,
- what improvement is required,
- by when,
- what will happen if the individual fails to comply.

This last point generally points out that the next step, if things don't improve, is a more severe warning, or even dismissal in disciplinary situations. It has an exact parallel in this assertiveness technique, in which you spell out the consequences of someone not changing their behaviour. This brings home the importance of working for a sensible outcome and gives everyone the opportunity to make adjustments before things get out of hand.

So, when the service engineer could get no sense from either the line or the functional manager, the consequence was that Hector, the director, was the next point of contact. Used this way it can be a fairly heavy approach, especially if not handled sensitively, and particularly when you're called on to use it upwards with those senior to you. In other situations it is more straightforward and clear, for example in this sort of scenario:

'To complete this job, Jim, we need that extra material you promised. If we don't get it we can't complete.'

or

'I have already told you that you must use the safety switch. If you don't do so you risk your own safety and that of others – and I will have no option but to issue a formal warning. I'd rather not have to.'

So spelling out the consequences may be a last resort option, in some cases. You may be able to use it more easily with those people reporting to you, but even then it may give the impression of a threat or blackmail, if it is used in an inappropriate manner or the wrong situation.

Trying techniques out in safety

Now that you have explored several techniques, some basic and others more specific, it's time to have a dry run and work out what could fit where. Looking at situations and testing your responses is a sound way of confirming that you can apply the techniques, build confidence and be reassured that you can do this.

We'll look at half a dozen common scenarios, some more major than others, in which one or more assertiveness techniques can make a real difference. They have been selected as examples that crop up in many people's lives, so you are very likely to recognise at least some of them from your own experience.

After you've had the chance to work out what you would do and say, there will be some comment to compare your ideas against. But there are no absolute right or wrong answers, so your approach may be better for you than the suggestions we make. The only thing to bear in mind is that the ABC technique rarely can be missed out. It's the basis of the whole approach.

Self-test 7.1

THAT CAN'T BE RIGHT ...

You're in a bar and you order a round of drinks. You expect it to come to around £6 but you get only a handful of loose change from a £10 note.

What would you do?

The passive approach is to say nothing, sit there fuming and feeling you've been ripped off. The aggressive way to tackle it is either to shout at the person who served you that they're trying to cheat you, or to make a very public show of stomping across to the price list with a pen and paper and doing the sum.

The assertive way of handling it is to:

- ask the bar attendant to come over, making sure your body language is appropriate, and you neither shrink down and look sheepish, nor bang on the bar and look furious;
- follow the ABC route and say:

  'I know you're busy but I'd appreciate a moment of your time. I'm not sure of your prices here, however £9.64 for the four drinks I just bought is more than I thought it would be. I'd like you please to just check it through for me.'

Put yourself in the shoes of the bar attendant and you'll see there's very little option but to check it, when the point is made like this. A customer making the point firmly but calmly leaves the bar attendant in a position where, if they have made a mistake, it can be acknowledged and rectified without a scene.

If, on the other hand, the amount is right and it's just an extremely expensive bar, you've haven't lost face either. You can just say thank you, sit down in the knowledge that you've dealt with an issue which could have eaten away at you and spoilt your evening ... and make a mental note to stay out of there in future.

Self-test 7.2

NOT AGAIN

Last year the boss 'asked' you to work late on the budget report that goes to the board each spring. It was a last-minute rush job, although the boss should have planned it weeks in advance.

You gave in and did it, even thought you were meant to be taking the family to the cinema as a birthday treat for one of the children. They went without you and you felt really bad about it.

Now it's happening again. You're being told that the budget has to be sorted out and you're needed at the office late this evening. It will mean missing the party.

What would you do?

You could always cave in again, of course. And you need to recognise that a blank refusal could make life very difficult in the long-run.

The first move is the ABC line, of course.

> *'I know it's urgent, however, I did it last year and you promised it wouldn't happen again. I am always happy to do my share as you know, but I have another commitment which I can't break, so I'd rather you found someone else this year.'*

But you're the only person available who knows about it ... so there is no one else. Maybe repeating the message will work, and stating feelings will have an effect?

> *'Yes, I recognise I have the clearest oversight of the issues, however, I did make sacrifice last year and I feel upset that it's happening again. I'd like to help, however, I have promised to be elsewhere, so I really can't do it.'*

Still no joy. The emotional pressure is starting to tell and you know that you're going to have to do at least part of this job. It's time for a compromise that will give you what you need, while providing the boss with a get-out.

> *'OK. I can see we're stuck. Even so, I have to leave at 5.30 as I already promised that. What I could do is to work on ideas at home, later tonight. Then we could both come in very early tomorrow and crack through it. When we've done the report incidentally, I'd like to spend time planning what we do next year, so we have more time to get this right in future. How does that sound?'*

If it's the best offer available, the boss is likely to grab it. It's not an ideal solution, but it is a practical compromise. It means the report gets done and it has one other major benefit as well. Acting assertively in this way makes it far less likely that you will ever be seen as a soft target again, and their respect for you will rise.

There's always an outside chance, though, that the boss is a total bully, acts entirely unreasonably and threatens you with the sack if you don't stay. This would have been the case whatever you said, and even if it does happen, there are real benefits from assertiveness. You will feel better about the way you handled yourself, and will have removed any belief that you are a doormat to be trodden down at will.

Self-test 7.3

PLEASE GO AWAY ...

Tim is one of those people who always seems to have the time to stop and chat ... even when it interferes with your own tight schedule.

He drops into your office frequently and starts a conversation, without any thought for what you're already doing. He's just done it again and you want him to leave.

What would you do?

This common difficulty starts to be resolved with the use of assertive body language. If you stand up and move towards the door, it sends a clear and unspoken message. It shows you're not just going to sit there and chat.

The ABC approach fits pretty well:

> *'I know that the traffic situation is awful, Tim. Trouble is I'm in the middle of putting together this bid that has to be finished by noon. I'd love to talk – but later. See you in the canteen about 12.30?'*

This isn't an overtly aggressive individual, so there's no anger to deal with. It's more of a nuisance than a threat; however, it is aggressive behaviour as Tim is doing what he wants at your expense, failing totally to take account of your needs and wishes. Therefore, you're completely entitled to throw him out ... but assertively, so there are no hard feelings.

Self-test 7.4

LATER ...

No sooner has Tim gone than one of your staff comes in with a problem – not a work problem, but a personal issue they want to talk through with someone.

You've always tried to have an open door for staff but just at this moment there's still that bid to finish.

You want to help and feel guilty that you ought to send him away. But if you don't the bid won't get done and you won't be able to concentrate on the employee's problem anyway.

What would you do?

The danger lies in giving in to the guilt and asking the employee to start opening up. This will throw your schedule, and you won't handle the employee sympathetically either. Even if you say all the right things, your body language will give you away, as you glance at your watch or the work on the desk, look worried and a little distracted, or try to speed up the counselling session.

Far better to come clean, and go for a solution that suits everybody.

> *'I can see this worries you. The problem is that at this moment I have something urgent to finish, and I probably wouldn't give you my full, undivided attention. I'd rather do that, because if it's important enough for you to come to me in confidence, it's important enough for me to treat you seriously.*
>
> *'If you come back at, say, half past three, I will block out half an hour and we can talk undisturbed. Is that a good time for you?'*

What a positive outcome! Not only does it solve your immediate problem, it makes the employee feel appropriately valued and special. They'd much rather you spent quality time with them later, than squeeze them in now and go through the motions just to look good. And there are very few problems that can't wait a couple of hours longer, if they're going to be handled with a more focused and constructive approach.

Self-test 7.5

I FIND IT OFFENSIVE ...

You're aware that a colleague makes fun of you behind your back, to other colleagues with whom you get on pretty well. She seems to think you're a studious individual, with no sparkle, and has coined the nickname 'the librarian', which you find offensive. (So would librarians, incidentally).

It has led you to feel awkward in her presence and you need to do something about it.

What would you do?

Most aggressive people who find it easier to channel their aggression through sarcasm and second-hand comments also find it awkward when their behaviour is challenged directly and assertively.

The simplest way to tackle this is to speak to her privately, using a mixture of ABC and stating feelings.

> *'I know you think I'm boring, and that you refer to me as "the librarian". I'm not sure what I've done to make you feel this way, and I have to say I find it offensive and quite hurtful. It would be helpful if we got on better and I'd like to find a way of doing that. If you have a problem with the way I work with you perhaps you'll tell me about it, so I can think about changing anything I do that is causing you a problem.*
>
> *'In any event, I'd like you to stop talking about me behind my back.'*

There may be a flurry of petulance as the offending party feels a bit embarrassed, but you should achieve the outcome you want. It will not only carry considerable weight with her, but also confirm to other colleagues that you are an individual with some self-esteem and self-confidence.

Self-test 7.6

COPING UNDER FIRE

Tim has just stormed into your office and started laying into you, verbally. It seems he's got the impression that you told the managing director that it was his fault, not yours, that the order for the new customer was wrongly addressed.

In fact, what you said was that the customer probably gave Tim's department the wrong details, and in any case, it's more important to find out how such mistakes can be prevented in future, rather than have raging arguments about the history of this one.

He starts off, 'Thanks for stabbing me in the back! Remind me to do the same of you sometime'. And then he goes on with the tirade without pausing for breath. When he does stop briefly you have the chance to say something.

What would you do?

Situations like this one can call for all the techniques to be used. The place to start is with the ABC:

> *'I can see you're upset because you think I told the MD it was your fault. I didn't though, and we don't normally sort out our differences like this, Tim. Take a seat and let's talk it through calmly.'*

He's wound up, though, so you may want then to cloud the issue:

> *'I can understand how you got that impression, and if I were in your shoes I may well feel the same.'*

or count to three and then state your feelings:

> *'If that were the real situation, Tim, I'd apologise. I didn't say that, and I'm disappointed you think I could have. Let's talk this through like we always do, because at the moment your anger really is stopping us getting this sorted out.'*

If he shows no signs of letting up, though, you may want to use further techniques, like stating the consequences:

> *'This is getting us nowhere. If we can't talk about it calmly I don't think there's any point in continuing for the moment, and we'll need to fix another time for a full discussion. However, I'd prefer to sort it out now, constructively.'*

Reviewing how you got on

■ ■ ■

As you went through the scenarios, the chances are your confidence grew and you could see effective ways of handling the situation. It isn't quite the same as doing it in real life, of course, but what you have done is recognise what you can do to raise your assertiveness level and come away with more constructive and positive results.

It's important to look back and review how you did, because that's how you can identify where you would have done well, and where you want to explore issues a little more deeply. This review and improvement process is something that needs to work not only here, but also in your practical use of assertive techniques in real situations.

Continuous improvement

Virtually all management issues, from quality to customer care, involve the use of monitoring, review and planning techniques, so that current good practice can be developed and areas that need enhancement can be worked on. Assertiveness is no different.

It's impossible to change and improve everything at once, which is why we have stressed that the place to start is with the ABC and then add to it. But even the way you use the ABC won't be perfect first time. You'll come away from situations knowing that you could have said something in a better way, or made slightly different points. The important thing is that you use this knowledge to enhance your performance next time, adding further success to what you did well the first time. If you come away knowing that something didn't quite operate as you had hoped, don't give up and say assertiveness doesn't work; plan marginal changes so you refine your performance for the future.

Any performance improvement – whether it's in individual appraisal, financial audit or health and safety risk assessment – is based on a simple and dynamic cycle. Knowing what happened is the starting point, but its only real use is as information that helps shape the future. The cycle looks like this.

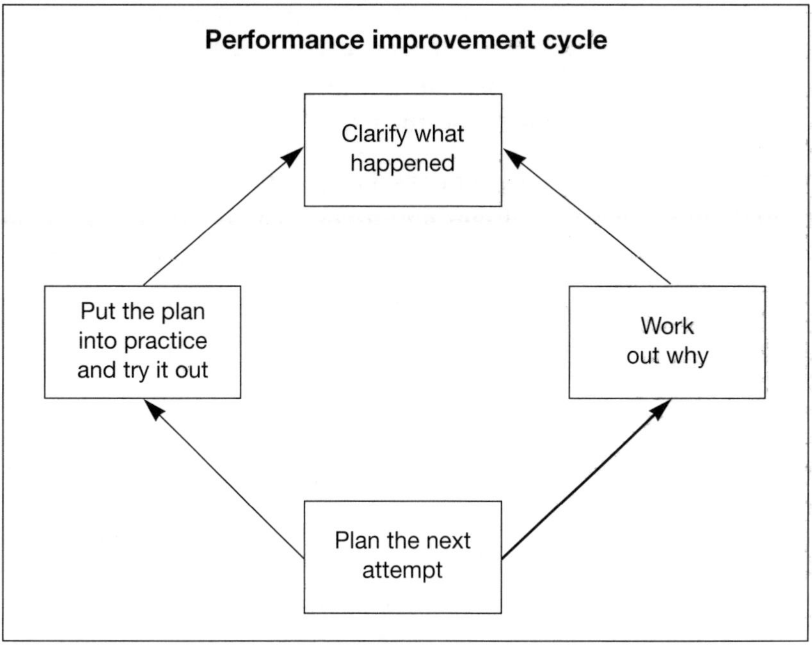

There are a few points that need to be made about the various stages in this cycle, specifically:

- Clarifying that what happened is about observable results and outcomes, not reasons.
- What happened could be effective or ineffective, or any shade of grey in between, but is always more than a list of problems and mistakes (in the same way as the basis for constructive feedback contains positives as well as negatives).
- Why it happened could be about your performance, or may be about other factors; when identifying improvements to your use of interpersonal skills such as assertiveness, focus on personal performance and what you did that worked well or badly.
- Planning the next attempt starts with a recognition of the positive outcomes, the things that worked that you want to do

again; that's just as important to the plan as a list of issues you want to change.

- If there are several things you want to change and improve, don't try to do them all in one go; select the most crucial points and work on just one or two – coming back to the others in future trios round the cycle.
- When planning improvements, be specific – focus on detailed and simple actions; if you found you lost control by reacting rather than responding, planning to count to three is a good way to go.
- Having tried them out, start the cycle again and review what happened.

In this way, improvements are a sort of helix, or corkscrew, continuously moving forward and building on existing success. When you've been working on improvements for some time, take an occasional longer look back and review all the improvements you've made. You'll be amazed at how apparently trivial changes have added up and improved your success, and just how far you have come in a short space of time.

One final point on this review process. Remember when we looked at feedback and said it helps because an onlooker often sees more of what is really going on? Well, it is possible to either kid yourself, or to see yourself differently from how others perceive you. It pays to get feedback from someone else:

- someone you trust to be honest,
- someone you will listen to and take notice of,
- someone who cares enough about you to give you their honest views,
- someone who understands (or will understand) the nature and power of the constructive feedback process,
- someone who is prepared to do it.

Planning for the future

Now you have explored:

- the need for effective assertiveness to be founded on beliefs about rights and responsibilities,
- basic patterns of aggressive, passive and assertive behaviour, both spoken and non-verbal,
- the effects of each behaviour pattern on you, other people and the results you seek,
- a foundation approach with the ABC technique, and more advanced techniques that build on it,
- how and where to apply techniques in different situations,
- the power of review and planning for continuous improvement.

The most effective way of ending your introduction to assertiveness is to plan initial improvements for yourself. Study the personal review and action plan that follows, and use it to take the first steps in developing your assertive approach. Remember to set achievable and realistic targets and not to aim for the impossible. Small steps get you there just as surely as giant leaps.

Putting your plans into action will stand you in good stead as you carry out your role in an increasingly stressful and competitive environment.

So, take some time to work through the following plan.

Checklist 7.1

PERSONAL REVIEW AND ACTION PLAN

I think I am currently:
(be honest and get feedback from others where possible)

❑ Aggressive ❑ Passive ❑ Assertive ❑ A mixture (explain)

The reasons I think this are that I ...
(use specific examples if it helps)

1 ______________________________

2 ______________________________

3 ______________________________

4 ______________________________

5 ______________________________

6 ______________________________

I want to make the following change(s) ...
(be clear and specific)

1 ______________________________

2 ______________________________

3 ______________________________

4 ______________________________

To achieve this I intend to ...

1 ______________________________

2 ______________________________

3 ______________________________

4 ______________________________

The things that will help me achieve this are:

1 ______________________________

2 ______________________________

3 ______________________________

4 ______________________________ ▶

The problems I will have to overcome are:

1 ______________________________

2 ______________________________

3 ______________________________

4 ______________________________

I will feel I have succeeded when ...

1 ______________________________

2 ______________________________

3 ______________________________

4 ______________________________

A final thought

■ ■ ■

If you are still with us, we ask you to read this final thought.

So, you have now finished the book and have had a really good grounding in the techniques of assertiveness. You have also completed a personal action plan which should help you to put many of the ideas in this book into action.

Finally, though, it is worth tying up a few thoughts and presenting a final window on assertiveness.

Assertiveness takes courage. It takes courage because many people shy away from their feelings and expressing them clearly and openly, and this is what assertiveness asks us to do. And it is for this reason that assertiveness is truly challenging. It challenges us to behave like grown-ups and leave the playground behind. It says that people can behave in a civilised way towards each other and that everyone *can* win as a result. And if you say this to an average bunch of people, you are bound to get voices that disagree strongly.

In this sense, it actually challenges some deep-seated and rather pessimistic views of the world – that good guys never really make it to the top and the strong always triumph over the weak. That the law of the jungle dictates the way organisations work. It challenges us to live our lives in a more thoughtful way and says that we should learn from our mistakes – always easier in theory than in practice. None of this is easy, especially if you have a boss from hell, or indeed staff from the same dark and dreary quarter.

Assertiveness actually asks us to look closely at ourselves and the way we think, feel and behave. You could argue: who wants to do that?

After all, we turn up at work to work, and not go through a journey of self-discovery. But this would be to miss the point. Assertiveness does help and the authors of this book are living proof of it.

But don't be fooled.

You read the books on assertiveness and it all looks easy – if not rather trite and superficial. And, as for those besainted souls that write the books, well! On the surface they seem like higher beings.

It will no doubt comfort you that we still find the difficult people difficult and the obnoxious ones, obnoxious. We still find passive people passive and we still find that life has a messy habit of upsetting our best plans. We also get angry, upset, prickly, unreasonable ... but only sometimes.

But assertiveness has helped us to be more effective, and we hope it will help you too. It hasn't solved our problems, but it has helped us to deal more effectively with people, and it's people who have a worrying tendency to cause the most problems.

And this final window on assertiveness is your own.

Please use the space to add your own window on assertivess.

Window 8

MY OWN STORY

Index

acid test 4

aggressive behaviour 47–48, 89
  assertiveness and, difference between 57
  effect of 48–53
  slowing down aggression 159

assertiveness,
  ABC of 97
  aggression and, difference between 57
  assertive thinking 176–178
  background to 1
  basics of 55
  definition of 2, 32
  further techniques 175–187
  getting started 91–92
  importance of 31
  making it work 173
  planning for the future 197–200
  putting it into practice 57–59, 110–115, 187–196
  quick fix, not a 35
  rights and responsibilities, understanding your 92–95
  right to be wrong 95–96
  spelling out the consequences 185–187
  stating feelings 178–181
  techniques, trying out, in safety 187
  what matters most 181–185

behaviour
  aggressive behaviour 47–48, 89
    effect of 48–53
  controlling your 156
  control, staying in 155–174
  extreme types of 2

frustration, avoiding 158–159
manipulative 53–55
passive or submissive 40–42
possum's law 44–47
slowing down the angry colleague 159–160

boss, handling the 113–115
choice, hierarchy of 96
knock-on effects 102

colleagues, dealing with 115–118

communication
body language 106–109
clarity of 9
clouding the issue 161–162
emphasis, repeating to gain 163
feedback,
constructive 167–172
giving, assertively 166–167
getting your message across 100–102
language 104–106
point of view, expressing your 78–81
repetition 164
techniques 165

conflict
aftermath of, handling the 61–62
culture of
performance difficult in 5
fight fire with fire 25
hidden sources of 19, 21–22
manager, with 66–68
obvious sources of 20–21
predictability of 2
reactions to, your 39–40
reasons for 25–26
cultural 25–26
gender 26
taking flight 24–25

talking and listening 27–28
understanding 25–28
unexpected, handling 84–87

control, staying in 155–174

disagreeing 81–84

don't know, saying you 81–82

emotions,
after an event 4
types of 3
environment, effect of 4

frustration, avoiding 158–159

Hades Incorporated 8–9

ideas, welcoming 10–11

knock-on effects 102–104

listening
first, then reacting 122–123
importance of 97–100

management style
assessing 76–78
aggressive behaviour 47–48
effect of 48–53
conflict, your reactions to 39–40
knowing your role 74
manipulative 53–55
passive or submissive 40–42
possum's law 43–47
understanding your 36–39

negotiating 125–153
agreeing a deal 150
continuous 130
clouding the issue 161–162
defining 127–128
fixed position 144–146

give and take 143–144
ingredients in 126–127
invitation to 140–143
mutual interests and trade-offs 128
outcomes of 132–134
perfect 153
preparation for 137–140
principled 146–150
process of 135–136
resolving conflict using 151
steps in 136
thinking it through in advance 157
winning or losing, feelings of 131

Nirvana Corporation 9–12

no, saying 18–19, 68–71, 119–120

organisational culture
aspects of 5
changing 6–8
effect on new staff 5
reflecting on your 14
you and 6
types of 6

people
types of 7–8
unpredictability of 3

personal development 6–8, 65–88
analysing your reaction 65–66
fear of dislike, conquering your 72–73
judging your approach 71–72
knowing your role 74

point of view, expressing your 78–81

praise,
accepting 122
giving 121

problems
  diagnosing 15–17
  effect of not facing 14
  understanding your own attitudes to 22–24

solutions, offering 120–121

teamwork, importance of 11–13

violence in the workplace 53